"Judith Bowman has penned the definitive guide to social and professional interaction. Striking at the heart of self awareness and emotional intelligence, Bowman provides a a step-by-step guide to social comportment for today's business executive seeking a competetive edge."
—*Matthew Power, President, Risk Specialists Management, Inc., AIG*

"This is the essential business guide for anyone in business, in the 21st Century."
—*Michael Nitti, Life Coach/Business Consultant & former Vice President, The Anthony Robbins Companies*

"A readable code of manners that's certain to provide a kindness edge to anyone involved in today's fast-paced, high-tech business world. **Don't Take The Last Donut** is loaded with good, sensible advice on how to make a good, lasting impression on others and feel good about yourself."
—*Bill Ketter, Vice President for News, Community Newspaper Holding Inc., and Senior Vice President Eagle-Tribune Publishing Co.*

"If you want to make a great and lasting impression, *Don't Take the Last Donut* provides excellent advice for a wide variety of social and professional settings. With specific examples, Judy Bowman reminds us that we should never underestimate the power of properly presenting and conducting ourselves in the course of developing successful relationships."
—*Steve Batza, Executive Vice-President, Liberty Mutual Group*

Don't
Take
the Last
Donut

NEW RULES OF BUSINESS ETIQUETTE

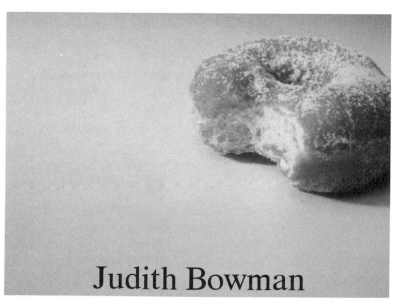

Judith Bowman

CAREER
PRESS
Franklin Lakes, NJ

DON'T TAKE THE LAST DONUT
EDITED BY AND TYPESET BY KATE HENCHES
Cover design by Mark Melnick
Printed in the U.S.A. by Book-mart Press

To order this title, please call toll-free 1-800-CAREER-1 (NJ and Canada: 201-848-0310) to order using VISA or MasterCard, or for further information on books from Career Press.

The Career Press, Inc., 3 Tice Road, PO Box 687,
Franklin Lakes, NJ 07417
www.careerpress.com

Library of Congress Cataloging-in-Publication Data

Bowman, Judith, 1953-
Don't take the last donut : new rules of business etiquette / by Judith Bowman.
     p. cm.
  ISBN-13: 978-156414-929-9
  ISBN-10: 1-56414-929-3
     1. Business etiquette. 2. Self-presentation. 3. Impersonal relations.
I. Title. II. Title: New rules of business etiquette.

HF5389.B69 2007
395.5'2--dc22

2006102988

Acknowledgments

No book emerges from the efforts of just one person. This one came together during many years and with the love and support of many individuals.

Thank you first to my family: my parents and my brothers. It was while growing up with my four siblings that it was made clear what being a true "gentleman" and "lady" were all about. It was during the family dinner hour where we all first learned "the rules" and the role they play in the smooth functioning of everyday life. As junior hosts and hostesses, we were taught valuable lessons in how to make others feel comfortable, warm, and at ease while in our home. The importance of family, the theme of "contributing," and treating others with respect and consideration were all engrained in us. These were valuable, indelible lessons, which have served me well.

Thank you to my many wonderful and valued clients and students, with whom I have made every mistake and faux pas and learned.

Thank you to Susan Flynn of the Eagle Tribune Publishing Company for taking a chance on me as a writer in 2000 by initiating the *Everyday Etiquette* column, which remains intact today. To Christine Gillette, my features editor, whose patience and support has been invaluable. I wish to especially thank Bill Ketter, my former editor in chief, currently vice president for news at Community Newspaper Holdings Inc. of Birmingham, Alabama, for his continued support, advice, and guidance. To Mike Nikitas, senior anchor, New England Cable News, for embracing our principles, and for promoting and hosting the then first-of-its-kind weekly etiquette feature "Etiquette First" and "Mind Your Manners" segment on New England Cable News, which ran for a combined total of four years.

To my agent, Lynn Sonberg, I offer heartfelt thanks for her vision and support of my dream to take all that I have amassed through the years and put it in book form. Thank you to my collaborating writer, Ellen Neuborne, for her help in preparing the manuscript. And thanks to Michael Pye and the talented team at Career Press for their skill and professionalism in embracing and marketing this book.

Ultimately, I would like to thank my grandmother, Helen Kerwin O'Connor, my "Yaya," who always believed in me and inspired me, and my mother, whom I always admired and sought to emulate because she is so gracious, beautiful, and elegant. I thank my aunt Helen O'Connor, "Auntie," who has also always believed in me, advised me, and encouraged me, for her unfaltering love, support, and prayers. My father, Ronald Bowman, who was himself self-taught, taught us everything he could and, without knowing it, inspired me. To John Maihos, my valued friend and business advisor, without whom nothing would happen in my business. To my son Bowman, who, when he entered this world, changed mine forever, and has inspired me to be all that I can be. To my fiancée, Jay, my soul mate and love of my life, who believes in me, inspires me, and supports and loves me no matter what.

Contents

Little Things Mean a Lot

Two consultants vied for a single lucrative client. To make the final call, the potential client had a business lunch with each contender.

Candidate A dressed for the lunch in khakis, brown tassel loafers with argyle socks, a casual sport jacket sans tie—a notch below that of his dining companion. He kept a laser focus on discussion of business matters during the entire lunch meeting. In his follow-up, he kept equally focused on getting business answers to all that had been presented and discussed at lunch.

Candidate B dressed a notch above his potential client in a well-tailored suit. Candidate B recognized his challenge and this opportunity to establish trust and to develop the relationship. He assumed nothing and did much to prepare for their time together. He arrived in advance at the restaurant, which he had selected after learning it was his prospective client's favorite. He requested a private table and specified seating arrangements with the wait staff, giving his client the best seat. He became acquainted with his wait staff's first names and the location of the rest rooms, and he made arrangements so the check never arrived at the table. He waited at the door, ready to greet his guest, and allowed his guest to enter and be seated first at the table. He ordered course for course with his guest with complete disregard of his own appetite. Discussion included family, vacation plans, summer activities, travel, an insignia pin worn on his lapel, and some light politics. They discussed business only to the extent that it emphasized his expertise and specific ways in which he knew he could help his potential new client.

After the lunch, he returned to his office and handwrote a three-sentence note. He used his high-quality monogrammed stationery, thanked this individual for taking the time to join him for lunch, and expressed his hope that they would have the opportunity to work together.

Assuming all other elements were equal, which consultant do you believe would win the business? We believe it would be Candidate B. Why? Candidate B paid attention to the nuances, the small ways in which he could distinguish himself and make his potential client feel valued and special. This attention to detail and nuances helps distinguish him from his competition and builds a connection of trust with his potential client.

Nuances are a powerful tool in business. It is not that courtesies enter into the conscious decision-making process. Few individuals award business because they are impressed with someone's manners. This anecdote illustrates an often unspoken element of the decision-making process: Actions, even small and seemingly insignificant, influence overall perception. Nuances are the clues that illuminate the greater self. They show an individual who takes the time, makes the effort, and goes to the trouble to consider and execute a myriad of details. They demonstrate attention to the little things, which shows genuine interest and respect. The recipient will notice and consider: What else does this individual take the time, make the effort, and go to the trouble to learn, practice, master, and execute? I want to do business with this observant, attentive, detail-oriented individual.

There is nothing little about the little things in business. The little things in business are not insignificant. More than a quaint display of good manners, business etiquette is a critical business tool. Business etiquette is a set of signals you send to show respect, inspire confidence, and earn trust in order to earn the right to advance the relationship. These are the pillars of success in the business world.

The good news is these nuances, the little things, are not as difficult to grasp as one might think and I have a system for identifying and managing them. I call the system the Four Cs: Confidence, Control, Contribution, and Connection. When you consciously and very deliberately practice and ultimately master each, it becomes part of you and your personal style. These nuances will distinguish you personally and professionally when executed with positive energy, genuine enthusiasm, and sincerity, which comes across through your body language, eye contact, and behavior.

Let us begin with *confidence*, which starts with believing in one's self. Confidence is all about projecting positive energy, a positive mental spirit, and a positive attitude. Confidence comes from within. Anyone can project an air of confidence. However, it takes much practice to master the many steps and nuances involved so that others perceive your actions and demeanor as sincere, credible, and authentic. If your actions are not genuine, you come across as forced, contrived, and unnatural. This will lead to a disconnect. It is imperative you rehearse, practice, and master these nuances and your confident demeanor so they become part of you and your personal style. The confident aura an individual does or does not exude will hinder or help foster the relationship going forward. Projecting confidence, or not, will ultimately make or break any business interview, meeting, relationship, or deal. Projecting positive energy, confidence, and control must be present from minute one in any successful business relationship.

When I enter a room to give a presentation, I demonstrate how this works. I present two similar opening remarks, each with distinctly different energy and word emphasis:

1. "Hi. My name is Judy. I am here today to talk about professional presence, how exuding confidence and paying attention to the little things will help distinguish you in business."

When I say this in a cordial yet unremarkable tone, with a lack of facial expression and dead eyes, I am typically met with group-wide glassy stares. Then I begin again. The second version projects confidence, authority, and high energy. I punch out the words with emphasis and make a few adjustments:

2. "Hello! My name is Judith Bowman, founder of Protocol Consultants International. We specialize in professional presence and nuances, ways in which professionals can further distinguish themselves in business."

The second version, enunciated with high energy, enthusiasm, and sincerity, genuinely projects my personal style and my signature. The second version uses words to convey my key emotional concepts. Most importantly, the second version projects my confidence and energy.

The second version is always well received. The group is immediately engaged. The room has a shared positive energy and participants now positively anticipate what is to follow. I see smiles, positive nods, and many in the group shift forward in their seats. I have their attention, which is not a surprising reaction. Confidence is attractive! Confidence and positive energy are what we as human beings are naturally drawn to. When we see someone who projects confidence and positive energy, we instinctively consider this to be a person with whom we want to connect.

An important element of confidence is maintaining consistency, even outside a business context. What if I met you on the street and said, "Hello, Jack, how are you?" and you responded, "Don't ask. My kids are sick, I had another argument with my wife, my car needs more work, and I think I may be getting laid off." I would have one impression of you. However, if I asked the same question and, despite all this, you responded, "I am fabulous; thank you for asking, Judy. How are you today?" I might have a different impression. My question is this: To which individual are you more drawn? Clearly, the second person, because confidence and positive energy are powerful draws. They are factors to be considered in advancing any relationship. The irony is the more you assume "the role" and project a positive attitude, the more you naturally become positive. "I think, therefore, I am" applies. Confidence and projecting positive energy are powerful.

Experienced business professionals have radar up for your confidence level from the very first handshake. They look at how you walk into the room, how you carry yourself, what you are wearing, and if you make eye contact or not. They notice the way you sit down and what you do with your hands. All this speaks volumes about you and sets the tone for your entire relationship.

Here is an example: As a former "Miss" (Teen Queen, Syracuse, New York), a former pageant coach, and now a judge in the pageant industry, I remember approaching one of the more seasoned judges after the first pageant where I coached contestants. I explained that I had been working with the contestants. I was befuddled about the process for selecting the winner. "How do you decide who is the best? I have been working with these women and they are all beautiful, bright, and talented. How do you decide?" This gentleman said, "Certainly, the interview process is critical; however, I know who the winner is the moment she walks through the door and sits down in front of me." He was talking about confidence, a presence, the way one projects and carries one's self. Attitude, demeanor, carriage, body language, and personal style all go into the mix. Inner confidence and beauty will project without one single word being said.

The pageant judge's view was instructive. Remember that in business and in life, we are constantly being judged. And this first impression, this first blush assessment and, hopefully, connection, provides valuable information about you to your prospect. Your ability to exude confidence, even though you may not be feeling it, is critical. Again, the many nuances, the little things, that combine to project this all-important first impression can mean everything.

Next on my list of Cs is *control*. I am often asked about who should initiate gestures such as a small talk, conversation, a handshake, or even seating. Many wonder if this should be based on age, rank, or gender. However, in business, generally speaking, none of these considerations are related to age, gender, company rank, or status. Rather, whoever initiates the handshake, the eye contact, or the conversation takes the lead and acquires control, which should be your goal throughout the relationship-building process. The person who has taken control then has the opportunity to remain in control throughout the meeting, covering everything from seating arrangements to the agenda, handling questions, objections, and more. You want to be that person who initiates, acquires, and maintains control. Control is all about focus. Control is about taking the initiative, setting goals, and maintaining structure to achieve your desired outcome.

You maintain control by being aware of the rules of engagement and knowing proper etiquette, such as when to initiate the handshake, how and when to make eye contact, how to make conversation, how to negotiate, handle objections and receive questions, and more. The way in which you endeavor to accomplish this earns trust and inspires confidence.

One powerful way to demonstrate control is in your choice of seating arrangements. Consider the judge in a courtroom venue who physically sits higher on a raised platform and in a larger chair than those seated in the courtroom. Those in the courtroom look up to the judge, who subtly looks down on those in the courtroom, while passing judgments. The judge's chair always faces the door, where he or she has full awareness of all incoming and outgoing courtroom activities in order to remain in the control seat. Courtroom seating arrangements are not accidental and the message is very subtle, yet strong.

When being seated in business, endeavor to identify and get the control seat—the one facing the door—for the same reasons as just stated. The more you exude control, the more purpose you convey to your business counterpart, earning trust, respect, and confidence.

Making this control move early in the relationship is key. I heard businesswoman Carolyn Kepcher speak once about the advantage she was able to take by initiating a control move. Ms. Kepcher is best known for her appearances on the *The Apprentice*. However, long before the cameras rolled, she was often the only woman at meetings within the Trump organization and, because she was a woman, traditional gentlemen colleagues deferred to her to enter the meeting room first, allowing her the opportunity to select her seat first. Ms. Kepcher made a control move by choosing the power position: the chair to Mr. Trump's right. It became "her" seat. The perception then was that Ms. Kepcher was Mr. Trump's most valued person. This perception was cast simply by taking this seat. Ms. Kepcher seized the moment and took control.

The third C is *contribution*. When you are invited anywhere, to a meeting, a social or networking event, or a symposium, you should go prepared to contribute to help make this event a success. Resist the urge to tap a colleague and say, "Let's go, put in an appearance for 15 minutes, and then we're out of there." This squanders a terrific opportunity. And if, in your 15-minute appearance, you make a beeline to the buffet table or to the bar, this sends the message that you are there to eat and drink rather than to contribute, meet, and mingle.

Please know that no one invites us anywhere in business because they believe we need to be fed. We are invited for one of two reasons:

1. As a way to say thank you for your business.
2. Because others believe you have something to contribute.

Indeed, it is our responsibility to help contribute to the overall success of the event and present ourselves in a positive light.

Growing up, my parents instilled in us the importance of contributing to everything, from the family dinner hour to social entertaining to conducting ourselves in the business arena. "To whom much is given, much is expected" was a theme ingrained in each of us. I am from a family of five children and, from when we were very young, we would gather at the dinner table and were expected to come prepared with topical conversation. We talked about anything from what we learned in school that day to questions we had about current events, or we shared an interesting book we were reading. We learned to listen as others spoke and to learn from them. We practiced making dinner conversation and how to ask open-ended questions. It was made crystal clear that we were expected to participate and contribute to this family time together. We all knew we did not come to the table simply to eat.

This important mindset carries into business as well. If you have been invited anywhere, it is because someone believes you have something to contribute to helping make their event successful. Be mindful of this and arrive prepared to step up and contribute. This is a little thing that will set you apart.

The final C is *connection*. In order to effectively relate to another, you need to connect with the other individual on every level. Connecting with another helps you to relate, builds trust, and inspires others to do business with you. There are many ways to create a connection; however, one of the most effective and often overlooked techniques is mirroring— becoming chameleonlike. Be sensitive to the other person's behavioral style including demeanor, voice, tonal quality, pace, inflections, word usage, and more, and seek to mirror that individual, not within the same second, but very soon thereafter. Generally speaking, it is imperative to be aware of your own behavioral style, and, as soon as possible upon meeting, assess the other person's behavioral style. Then, adapt so as not to clash, and work to form a firm foundation for the relationship.

I experienced a challenge wherein I was able to adapt my behavior to successfully establish a connection, thus forming a sound foundation with a new client. All this, without saying one word!

After much effort, I finally was granted a meeting with a gentleman who owns several radio stations. I wanted to explore any interest he may have had in a syndicated radio series and really wanted this meeting to go well. I was ultimately successful in making contact through the mutually respected third party and getting the appointment. However, when I arrived, there were some immediate barriers in place.

My host greeted me with a stiff, outstretched handshake, keeping me at arm's length—a physical barrier. He then invited me into his office and asked me to be seated. The only option was to sit across from him. I permitted him to be seated first and then I sat. I regarded his body language as he leaned back in his large, overstuffed chair and folded his arms in front of him, keeping his upper body closed, and crossed one of his legs by rooting his left ankle up on his right knee, yet another "closed" signal and a barrier between us. The meeting had not even begun and there were already abundant barriers between us.

I was seated across from him, in my protocol-correct professional sitting position, focused forward with the straight of my back and the back of the chair forming a "V." I focused my attention forward, toward my host. Awareness of the correct professional sitting position is a hallmark in appropriate business etiquette. I was sitting two-thirds of the way back in my chair, focused forward, to indicate interest with my body language. My legs sloped correctly to the right and my hands, resting hand over wrist, were on my knees. I was perfect.

However, as I read his "closed" body language, I knew I had to make some sort of change or the barriers would remain up and no business would be conducted. I thought, "How can I break down these barriers so that I can begin to connect with this gentleman?"

I embrace the premise: The beauty in knowing the rules is knowing when it is okay to break them. And so I broke the rules. I shifted my position and leaned back in my chair. I put my feet out in front of me and my hands came down, dangling by my sides.

As I moved, he responded. He put his crossed foot down, and then uncrossed his arms. He sat forward in his chair and then picked up his pen. I then sat forward, asked permission to take a few notes, assuming nothing during the relationship-building process and showing the utmost respect. He said yes; finally, we were relating. The meeting proceeded positively.

What made this meeting successful? My ability to read and interpret behavioral styles, knowing when it is okay to break the rules in order to ultimately connect and mirror body language and behavior. If I had not put these little things into play, chances are I never would have gotten past his barriers and arm's length mentality. All my good business ideas and propositions would have fallen on deaf ears. By mirroring and adapting in order to connect, I was able to secure an opening in this gentleman's mindset, advancing the meeting, the relationship, and the deal.

Failure to connect and mirror can cost you business.

Here is another story to illustrate how mirroring can influence a deal. I once had lunch with an individual whom I was considering hiring as a public relations consultant. I traveled to New York for this meeting, which this individual arranged at a very upscale restaurant. I was very eager to have this meeting as this person had come very highly recommended.

However, when we first met, there was failure to connect. This individual was not dressed professionally and wore zero makeup. While I was in high gear, Type A mode, she was very laid back in her attire, demeanor, and delivery. She spoke so slowly that I found myself finishing her sentences. Rather than reading me and adapting to my pace, my energy level, and my body language to win my business, she was frustrating and annoying me. We clashed. As a result, not only did we not connect, but not one word of business or pleasure was further discussed.

Mirroring is hardly a new concept. Ben Franklin was famous for his ability to adapt to the styles and surroundings of his associates. When he visited the Midwest or Philadelphia, he would dress the part, wearing burlap clothing and warm hats to fit in. However, when he traveled to Great Britain, his clothing style shifted and mirrored that of the highest nobility. In so doing, he paid a subtle compliment to his hosts and offered unspoken respect for them, their personal style, and their culture. He conveyed, through the nuances of his dress, that he understood where he was and with whom he was speaking. He understood that in order to successfully relate to others, in order to successfully connect, one must become chameleonlike, mirror.

In addition to the Four Cs, another subset of little things falls under personal style. Personal style is something that alone will not get you anywhere; however, combined with these other skills, will help you rise a notch above and truly distinguish yourself socially and in business. However, until you master and "own" all of the many nuances, which are actually steps that need to be rehearsed and practiced until they become part of you and your personal style, manifesting these nuances alone will come across as forced, contrived, and unnatural, and there will be a disconnect. Developing one's personal style requires study. Look to those whom you admire. How do they dress, carry themselves, speak, sit, treat others? Developing one's own personal style takes much practice, determination, and will. Understanding your persona is tantamount to exhibiting confidence and inspiring trust in order to connect.

Personal style is more than just the clothes you wear. It also refers to your demeanor, the manner in which you present yourself to the world. It is the "self" as others see you, and perception is reality. Repetition is reputation in this business of life, socially and professionally. Crafting a compelling message and a strong sense of self will speak volumes about you and your personal style. Learning how to integrate all of the many nuances together in order to become a part of your personal style while putting other people at ease is an art. Projecting positive energy, enthusiasm, and sincerity in your demeanor and personal style are undercurrents that will propel your positive perception as well as enhance your overall message and efforts.

Ultimately, your personal style, all these "little things" we discuss in this book, must be practiced. They are not just for when you think you need to call upon your most formal or professional demeanor. They need to be part of your regular habit, so practiced and so ingrained that they become a part of you and your personal style.

Nuances are also critical when the meeting is taking place in your office. Here is a quick list of little things that can mean everything when receiving a visitor:

☞   Close your office door after you invite someone in.

☞   Do not answer your phone during the meeting; place it on call forward.

☞ Do not sign papers, check e-mail, or attend to any other office task while the visitor is in your office.

☞ Initiate some small talk prior to conducting business.

☞ Ask visitors about themselves—their travel, family, and so on—in order to help put the other person at ease and grow the relationship.

☞ Prearrange seating in your office so that you are in the "control" seat and there are no barriers between you and the person with whom you endeavor to connect. Arrange seating so you sit corner to corner rather than across from your visitor, unless you are still evaluating this individual as a prospective client.

☞ Note powerful signals from the person's body language. Connect and mirror, or make the choice to break the rules in order to create the connection.

☞ Speak on their level, matching pace, word use, tone, and inflections.

☞ Be sure you are level to level while seated and standing unless you want to use your height, for example, to intimidate the other person.

☞ Hosts should make offers of hospitality, such as water or coffee; however, the savvy professional should graciously refuse such offers. Spilling will not enhance your reputation or grow the relationship in a positive way.

None of the above nuances alone are considered major; however, when added together, they will help create the professional, respectful tone of your meeting. They are small ways in which you can help place your visitor at ease, show respect, and begin to cultivate a feeling of trust between you and this individual in order to grow the relationship.

Little things can also play a role when calling on a client:

- ☞ Go to the rest room first, to check everything.

- ☞ Present your business card to the receptionist.

- ☞ Stand in the reception area, carrying your briefcase or portfolio in your left hand, leaving your right hand free to shake hands.

- ☞ Allow your host to lead to the meeting room.

- ☞ Be sure everything with you has to do exclusively with this client. Resist the urge to carry your largest briefcase to this client meeting, which gives the perception that they are one of "many" rather than your "one and only."

- ☞ Allow your host to be seated first.

- ☞ If you have the choice of being seated across from your host or angular, choose angular if you want to grow the relationship.

- ☞ If you are given a choice of seating and you want to exude control, choose the seat facing the door. A person of honor is seated to your right and copresenters are seated across from you, so that together you can "control" the room and meeting.

- ☞ Exchange business cards before the meeting and keep them with you, subtly placed around your portfolio so you can effectively use the cards.

- ☞ Introduce instead of announce each meeting participant.

- ☞ Provide an agenda.

☞ Choose your words carefully. For example, say "hello" rather than "hi," "I believe" rather than "I think," "however" rather than "but." Use more professional, hardworking words and word tracks.

Talking about doing the little things is easy. Practicing them requires awareness at all times. Be aware of what your own voice sounds like. If you do not know already, practice with friends and family, or try recording your voice. Practice sounding confident and projecting positive energy. Otherwise your tone and delivery may sound weak or disingenuous. One must also practice maintaining control, connecting, and mirroring in order to make the connection and have these little things appear seamless and natural. Like magic tricks, if the effort is obvious, the illusion is lost and the audience is disappointed, even annoyed at the attempted manipulation.

Some of the most successful people in the world, people who are truly world-class individuals, work long and hard to acquire these skills. Bill Clinton, one of the most charismatic, sought after, and well-paid public speakers in the world, spent many years practicing his craft. When he was governor, he often drew criticism and ridicule for his bumbling. However, over the years and after many rounds of practice and faux pas, President Clinton has honed his skills to the point where he is magnanimous and able to put virtually anyone at ease, inspire trust, and create the connection.

Other world-class individuals acquired their skills through many years of practice. Jacqueline Kennedy was coached meticulously, not only when she became First Lady, but throughout her upbringing and adulthood, regarding nuances and the elements of style. Princess Diana spent six days each week, 10 hours per day, for one year being coached before making her first public appearance as a member of the Royal Family. Both these women are considered paragons of grace, style, and class. And both practiced their craft with fierce and deliberate dedication, determination, and forethought. Little things may be little; however, they never come without effort.

Ultimately, everything you do in business has an impact. The savvy professional will remember that while executing on the major plays—networking, meetings, negotiations, travel— it is the little things, the nuances, strategically put into play that will distinguish one in business, build trust, and help grow the relationship. Indeed, these nuances will have a significant impact and help determine whether or not future business is conducted.

2

Introductions

You are at a networking event with a prospective new client and a long-time customer when the situation takes an unexpected turn. The CEO of your company decides to stop by and say hello. Although the long-time customer has been with your firm for many years, he and your CEO have never met. You also want to introduce the prospective new client. You rise to make the introductions.

Question: Whose name do you say first?

Answer: Always say the name of the most important person first.

In this case, the prospective client's name is said first. Although your loyal customer is clearly the most important, out of respect, say your prospective new client's name first and later be sure to thank the longtime customer for understanding. Say the name of the CEO last because without customers and their business, there would be no company, hence, no CEO. This done, you can be confident you have properly executed a formal business introduction.

Many people are simply unaware that a business introduction is, in fact, quite different from a social introduction.

Understanding this difference is important. When executed properly and with confidence, appropriate introductions can distinguish you positively and propel your career. You may find yourself in several roles during an introduction: You may be the individual providing the introduction, or you may be one of those being introduced. Either way, the rules will help you handle any situation with confidence and distinguish yourself. Your goal is to facilitate a positive connection between two individuals. Take this role seriously and use appropriate tools. Introductions may seem casual compared to other business interactions; however, they are in fact critical moments that set the tone for a business relationship.

Social introductions are simple: You say the name of the most important individual based on age or gender and make sure to mention something they have in common. You offer a level of enthusiasm regarding the opportunity to provide the introduction through your body language, energy, and the tone of your voice. "Sarah, this is my friend Jack. Jack, this is Sarah. Sarah used to be my manager at XYZ Company and Jack and I were classmates at Boston College. I'm so happy to finally introduce you to one another. And you have something in common: You are both avid runners." Then you are free to make your graceful exit and your work is done.

Business introductions require more heavy lifting. There is a form, a process, and a protocol to the business introduction. When done properly, you will shine as a result.

The first step to executing a proper business introduction is to know the form. Say the name of the more senior individual first: "Mr./Ms. Senior Individual...." If you only remember one thing about introductions, this is it. The primary rule governing proper business introductions: Always say the name of the most important person first. Then say, "May I introduce to you" (professional phrasing) or "May I present to you" (the more formal phrasing) and then say the name of the less senior individual. Then, offer something that will facilitate conversation between the two: "I understand you both have children applying to college this year," or "I understand you are both golf enthusiasts."

Each element of that form is important. Knowing which individual's name to say first is a critical part of a correct business introduction. By following appropriate protocol and saying the more senior individual's name first, you put both individuals at ease by making clear their status and their relationship. Using proper phrasing underscores the importance of the introduction by clarifying the moment, holding the attention of both parties, and connecting the two individuals, which provides the professional attention this proper business introduction deserves. Finally, it is your responsibility as the introducer to ensure the conversation between the two individuals gets underway. A topic that is not business related is often the best choice, and so a little pre-event research may be necessary.

The form of the introduction is just the bare outline of what you can do with this moment. There are many other nuances involved in executing a strong introduction. And, the more polished you are at this skill, the more you will shine.

Nuances of a Proper Business Introduction

Use honorifics. In business, unless otherwise instructed, women are "Ms." and men are "Mr." If a woman says specifically she prefers "Mrs." then by all means, respect her wishes. Note: Miss and Master are generally reserved for children. If the individual holds a degree that warrants an honorific such as Dr., Chancellor, or Professor, they are appropriate to use. Politicians and dignitaries from other countries—sheiks, princes, dukes, prime ministers, ambassadors, presidents, senators, and so on—will have honorifics and these vary from country to country. Whenever possible, research the correct form of address and introduction before the introduction. If this is not possible or you are in doubt, ask a mutually respected third party for advice. And if that is not possible either, do not guess: Ask your guests how they prefer to be addressed, announced, and introduced. When in doubt, err on the side of formality and be sure whatever you say is partnered with sincere body language, eye contact, and a genuine smile.

Be consistent. Like a scale, a proper business introduction must balance. If I say, "Dr. Tim Johnson, may I present to you..." then the next words out of my mouth must include an honorific, a first name, and a last name. The two must be in sync. If they are not, the introduction slights one of the individuals. Consider this example:

"Dr. Tim Johnson, may I introduce to you Ms. Smith."

What do you hear in that introduction? It implies that I have forgotten Ms. Smith's first name.

Suppose you really have forgotten the first name of one of the individuals. Do not panic. Just be sure the two phrases match. "Dr. Johnson, may I introduce to you Ms. Smith." The two are in sync. The introduction is correct.

Prioritize your players. It is important to say the name of the most important individual first. However, who is the most important individual in the introduction? That is not always easy to determine. Often, this can be understood by rank: The higher-ranking individual is the more important person in the introduction and you say that individual's name first. However, other pairings can get more complicated.

Some examples:

☞ When introducing a customer to the CEO, whose name is said first? In this case, the customer's. Without the customer, there would be no business and no CEO.

☞ When introducing your spouse to the CEO at the holiday party, whose name do you say first? The CEO's. Not because your spouse is less important to you, but because this is a company party and you want to show respect. Be sure to explain this to your spouse prior to the event, to maintain peace on the home front.

☞ Suppose the two individuals are equal in rank? You may use age to determine the order of introduction; the elder is introduced first. Or you may use gender; the woman's name is said first. Both are considered appropriate in a business setting.

☞ When introducing a governor or other high-ranking government official to your CEO, whose name is said first? Answer: the governor's. Any elected official outranks anyone in the private sector.

☞ Suppose your job is to introduce one very senior person to a room full of people, 10 or more individuals. My personal shortcut for handling this type of situation is to say the name of the senior person and then invite the individuals in the room to say their own names and titles. This is perfectly correct and a good way to avoid an error.

The biggest challenge to many people in any introduction situation is remembering names, which is central in the business world. Yet this is the most important take-away from any introduction. Therefore, when making an introduction, it is your responsibility to really punch out the names in a clear, concise way. Do not rush through a name, particularly a challenging one. Take your time. Also, be sure the names stand out in the introduction itself. To make this happen, say each individual's name first and then provide identifying information. "Mr. John Smith, may I introduce to you Ms. Sarah Anderson. Mr. Smith is considering using our firm's services. Ms. Anderson is our new senior vice president of marketing, and I understand you are both Boston College alums." By arranging the introduction in this way, you have queued up the names of each individual in such a way as to be easily heard and remembered.

When you are one of the individuals being introduced, focus on the name. As soon as you hear the other person's name, say it. Repeat it. Use it in conversation and use it often. Say the person's name as well as their honorific as you extend your hand for a handshake. Remembering names is not easy; however, if you can use the name right away, you have a far greater chance of keeping it in your head for future use. Finally, names can be used in parting as well. When separating after an introduction and some small talk, use the individual's name in your farewell. You will part with a positive impression.

Remember to project energy. Introductions can be challenging and require effort. However, when you are making introductions, you owe it to yourself and individuals involved to project energy and enthusiasm. Give parties the impression and feeling that you are pleased and honored to connect them. Allow them to feel as though they and their meeting are very special and not simply a random encounter. Set the tone of this introduction by providing a proper, professional power launch.

Key Physical Moves

Introductions are not just about what you say. They are also about what you do—where you place yourself, your hands, the way you stand, and other nuances during the introduction. Where you are in the moment can have a great impact on the success of the introduction itself. For example, the most important person should stand to the right of the introducer. When you are providing an introduction, this arrangement is important, even if it requires a bit of maneuvering on your part. Repositioning yourself will demonstrate to those present that you understand and are making your best effort to demonstrate respect and execute proper protocol for the introduction, which can only work in your favor. This is one nuance to the overall introduction that places you in a positive light.

Offer your hand. There are no gender considerations when it comes to the business handshake. Acquiring control early on in the relationship should be your goal. Therefore, initiate the handshake, and take control during this first moment of encounter.

Stand when being approached while at a dinner, for example. As a guest or host at a large gathering, expect many visits and introductions during the course of the evening. Be sure to rise whenever a visitor arrives or an introduction takes place. If you are seated at the dinner table hosting clients, for example, and an individual approaches you to make an introduction, rise from your chair out of respect to shake hands and acknowledge the effort in approaching and attempting to make the connection.

If the introduction occurs in your office, come out from behind your desk to shake hands. Many people forget this and simply reach across the desk for the handshake. This barrier between the two individuals remains and they are not fully connecting during this introductory moment.

If the introduction occurs outside, remove your sunglasses and/or gloves. Only the Queen of England has protocol's permission to shake hands wearing gloves. The rest of us must remove our gloves to shake hands, even if it is 10 below! On sunny days, remove your sunglasses so that your eyewear does not create a barrier between you and the individual to whom you are being introduced. Should you have the luxury of wearing eyeglasses selectively, do make direct visual contact and remove eyeglasses when first introduced; wear and use eyeglasses after the introduction.

Suppose you want to meet someone at a networking event or party. Other than a simple self-introduction, how can you facilitate an introduction? There is one very effective way to accomplish this. Enlist the assistance of a mutually respected third party. I was able to meet President George Bush (41) in this way. I was attending a meeting of the World Affairs Council and by chance my table was near that of President Bush. I happened to see someone I knew speaking with the president and later asked if he would introduce me to President Bush. He said yes and we walked over to the president's table. President Bush was the picture of proper decorum as he noticed we were approaching, graciously excused himself from his guests, and stood to shake my hand. In this case, the mere presence of the mutually respected third party was all that was required when I introduced myself to President Bush. President Bush then asked me several open-ended questions all about my business and me. He remained standing for the duration of our conversation together, perhaps two or three minutes. Then he shook my hand again as we parted. He made me feel so incredibly special and taught me an invaluable lesson about the power of proper and gracious introductions.

If no third party is present or available to facilitate the introduction, try making eye contact with the individual you would like to meet and assess if his or her body language invites approach and a self-introduction. For example, at a networking event or cocktail gathering, you may see an individual you would like to meet in conversation with another. Walk past slowly. It is possible that the person is not actually engaged, but is instead "stuck." By walking past slowly, you allow the person the opportunity to disengage by stopping you and providing the opening for you to introduce yourself.

Pitfalls and Responses

When something does go wrong in an introduction, there are several ways to finesse the situation.

Challenge: You have forgotten an individual's name.
Solution: You have several options.

Your first choice is to confess. Say, "I am so sorry. I have completely blanked on your name." Say this with honesty and sincerity and chances are you will be forgiven. Most people find remembering names a huge challenge. We have all been there.

Other options: You can ask another individual at the gathering to refresh your memory. You can ask to exchange business cards with the individual whose name you have forgotten. Proper etiquette suggests one should always ask if one would like your card and ask if you may have theirs, assuming nothing in this relationship-building process.

You can attempt what I call "The Set Up," which is when you send another individual over to introduce himself to the person whose name you have forgotten. Spouses will often do this. When people forget an individual's name, they may ask their spouse to approach that person and introduce himself as a way of getting the individual to say his or her name. This often works well. We are all conditioned to respond with our own name when someone offers his or hers. You do not need to be married to execute this tactic. A trusted colleague can also play "The Set Up" role.

What can you do to avoid this situation? Entire books have been written on ways to improve your memory in a business situation. There are several techniques to help remember names. You can try an association. If you meet an individual named Bill Scott you might associate that person with another Scott you already know who also wears glasses or who has curly hair. Be careful that any association you make, even in your own head, is not inappropriate or embarrassing. That could be, at best, distracting.

Another name remembering technique: Say the name of the individual right away and make an attempt to use that person's name more than once in conversation. If you can say the name three times during the course of the conversation, chances are good you "own it." There are many easy and unobtrusive ways to do this. Say the name immediately when introduced, make a mental association, ask for the person's business card, make another visual association, use the name during the course of conversation and again when departing. Ask them how they prefer to be addressed, which gets you their name again, too. Ask them to spell their name. Be careful when they say S.M.I.T.H.!

Because names are such a challenge, please be sensitive to the fact that others may forget yours. If you sense you are being "Set Up," play along and offer up your name clearly and audibly. Again, we should all be conditioned to respond by saying our name, slowly and distinctly, and to make an association in order to help others remember it. Never respond to a person who has offered a self-introduction with "I know who you are," as has happened to me in the past. This is not nice!

If name badges are used, be sure to wear yours high and to the right. That puts it in the sight line of anyone trying to read your name while shaking your hand. Do not clip your badge on your breast or down by your belt buckle, as this can be embarrassing for anyone looking long enough to commit your name to memory. Be sensitive. Names are not easy.

Challenge: You are about to introduce a very senior individual to guests. However, the senior individual is not standing to your right.

Solution: Make the effort to subtly maneuver yourself into proper positioning, even if this requires a light touch on the elbow or shoulder of the individual to indicate your maneuver. This may seem staged; however, it is a clear sign to everyone present that you appreciate and respect introduction protocol and that you are making every effort to ensure the introduction goes smoothly. Far from seeming fussy, your attempts at proper positioning will put players at ease. Ultimately, this will signal to others that they are in the hands of a knowledgeable, respectful professional.

Challenge: You introduce two people who already know each other.

Solution: Clearly, you should have been stopped long before the introduction went forward. It is not even nice to stand by while another person makes such an egregious error. However, should this happen to you, as it has to me, smile and make a positive statement about the situation. As always, humor helps.

Challenge: You have carefully researched the proper form of address to use with a visiting dignitary. However, the individual has arrived with a female companion whose status or relationship is not clear and you are not sure how to address and present this individual during introductions.

Solution: Given the event is already underway, and there is no time to research, quickly enlist the assistance of the mutually respected third party. However, your best bet is to be direct and quietly ask in advance, "How do you prefer to be addressed and introduced?" If you ask with sincerity, much is forgiven as you will demonstrate your desire to be appropriate and respectful.

Challenge: You are in a group at work when a senior manager approaches with an important customer in tow. The manager introduces the customer to other members of the group but inadvertently overlooks you. What do you do?

Solution: This is a faux pas on the part of your senior manager. However, you must use tact and discretion to rectify this. Do not roll over and give up. Rather, wait for an opening, such as eye contact from the client, then extend your hand and introduce yourself quickly and succinctly. Adopt an air of confidence, warmth, and professionalism.

Challenge: You have just been introduced to someone. Should you use that person's first name?

Solution: Avoid the temptation. Immediately using a first name is potentially self-sabotage. When in doubt, ask, "How do you prefer to be addressed?" which is far better than saying, "May I call you Bill?" Suppose the individual prefers William or Billo or Willy? The fact is the latter is a complicated question. How an individual prefers to be addressed is a question that covers more than just the use of first and last names. For example, you may be introduced to a woman whose name is Elizabeth Anderson. How does she prefer to be addressed? She may prefer Elizabeth, or, Liz, Beth, Betsy, Liza. The list goes on. Or perhaps she prefers to use her honorific, which may be Dr. or Chancellor or Professor. The possible permutations and combinations are such that there is no safe way to guess and, as always, assume nothing during the relationship-building process. Formality, sincerity, and being conservative will always win you respect and appreciation.

Challenge: You are called upon to introduce your manager to another individual. However, you sense the word "boss" sounds crude and tacky. How should you refer to this individual during the introduction?

Solution: Introduce both individuals, using their full names and titles. In this way, the fact that the person has seniority in your department suggests you work for them and will be evident without requiring you to state the obvious. Be sure your introductions match: honorific, first, and last name for each individual.

Challenge: You are preparing to attend a business function wherein you expect you will be required to make several important business introductions. You are nervous and not sure you will do everything right.

Solution: Forge ahead. Proper business introduction skills require practice and are not skills that come naturally to most people. Business introductions require remembering many things simultaneously, thinking on your feet, and effectively dealing with unexpected situations. You may have to smooth over a process if it is not going well. However, there is no way to acquire these skills without practice. You can read, study, and internalize all the rules and formulas you like; however, to use them effectively in a business setting, you need to practice. If you feel you are still honing your business introduction skills, you can help ensure your success by being sincere and erring on the side of formality. The respect you demonstrate will play a significant role in your overall success.

Sometimes even in a difficult introduction, one can come up with a brilliant moment. I had the occasion once to introduce the president of a major magazine to the president of a major car dealership. I had absolutely no idea what neutral topic I could inject to help launch these two individuals into conversation. So I had to think on my feet. I said each name properly and clearly, with titles, honorifics, and company affiliations, and then I said, "And it is clear you are both brilliant captains of industry." Both men beamed, shook hands, and conversation flowed easily between them.

Is there ever a case when one should break the rules of the introduction process? Yes, those situations do arise. For example, I once had the opportunity to introduce a woman in her 40s to a gentleman, currently in business, who was formerly a retired general. I thought, "Who is more important? Whose name should I say first?" Protocol suggests that the general's name should be said first. However, I knew this gentleman and knew he would object to this line of protocol. As a traditional gentleman in the truest sense, I knew he would always defer to gender. Therefore, I broke the rules and said the name of the woman first, which was appropriate for this specific introduction. Given that our goal is to put the two parties at ease and facilitate their meeting, if you know preferences of the individuals involved, it is appropriate to breach the rules of protocol to accommodate.

Finally, please bear in mind that when it comes to executing proper business introductions, erring on the side of formality and respect is key. One of the loveliest introductions I have ever personally experienced occurred when I was in the audience of a Paul McCartney concert in Boston. The lights were dimmed, the sound system came to life and the speaker began: "Ladies and gentlemen, may I introduce and present to you, Sir Paul McCartney." Use of both the business professional and formal phrasing together with Paul McCartney's very special honorific, Sir, made the moment that much more special for the thousands of us on hand to hear him sing and watch Sir Paul McCartney perform that evening. I believe the entire audience felt as though we had been properly introduced. And, this introduction set the tone for a truly magical evening.

How to recover if...
...you forget someone's name.

1. Confess. This is the most appropriate, most honest, and most positive way to recover. Remember, it's not what you say, rather, how you say it. Therefore, be sure to express sincerity and warmth. Say, "I am so sorry. I have completely blanked on your name."

2. Ask the person to please repeat his or her name. If the person provides first and last, you might say "Oh, I knew it was Jack, but Jack Anderson." Now you have both.

3. Ask the person how he or she prefers to be addressed. This allows you the opportunity to hear the name again.

4. Ask the mutually respected third party.

5. Ask for the person's business card; make a visual association.

6. Ask the person how to spell her name.

7. Try "The Set Up." Send a "Set Up" person over to introduce himself and then report back to you.

3

Small Talk

You arrive at the location of an off-site meeting and you are ushered into your client's office. As you are seated in the visitor's chair, your client takes a last-minute phone call that lasts longer than a few seconds.

Question: Should you sit still and wait or is there something you can do at this moment that will help ease some of the initial awkwardness and segue into a successful meeting?

Answer: After the silent signal gesture is made to "Please stay. I'll be with you in just one minute," it is okay to get up and walk around the office. Look at office décor, artwork, photos, and diplomas. Anything displayed in the office is okay to look at and fodder for small talk. Please note: Should you do not want others to ask, it should not be out. This is also an opportunity to learn more about this individual on a personal level, to enhance the relationship.

Look for your best possible item to make a connection with your client. Select whatever you feel you can most comfortably discuss. Be sure to avoid assumptions. (One client recently shared with me the story of one of his managers commenting on a photo. "When did you meet X person [a gentleman sports broadcaster]?" When asked to what he was referring, the manager pointed to the photo he believed to be the client and the gentleman sportscaster. To which the client replied, "That's not X, that's my wife.") Ask open-ended questions that allow your counterpart to share, thereby enhancing your relationship.

By initiating questions, several things are accomplished: (1) you initiate, secure, and maintain control, which is your goal; (2) you take the spotlight off you and your arrival; and (3) you are afforded the opportunity to hear the other person's voice first, and gauge their demeanor. By listening to the person's voice, you can glean valuable information. You can hear agitation, arrogance, trepidation, boredom, ill-health, or confidence. All these clues allow you to position yourself to either adapt to their style. By engaging in a few minutes of nonbusiness-related small talk you establish the tone. You also build connection and trust before getting down to facts and figures, dollars and cents. This is the art of small talk. Small talk is perhaps the most poorly characterized element in the business environment. This very common expression grossly misrepresents its own significance, for how can any conversation so critical, so vital, so challenging, be called "small"?

More often than not, we tend to dismiss small talk as just aimless prattle, something to fill in pauses and down time. Most do not use small talk to their advantage. Americans in particular are challenged by this. We are a nation of fast-talkers. Time is money. We feel a need to get to the point. However, small talk is not disconnected from the world of business at all. In fact, small talk is the prelude. It is the setup for what will become the smooth transition into the business conversation. The better you are at small talk, the better you will position yourself when business discussions begin.

In broad terms, small talk is the initial conversation you have with a fellow business professional that has nothing to do with business. Small talk may occur during the few minutes you have to chat before a meeting gets underway. It may be the words exchanged when meeting at a networking event or a business conference. It may be the discussion in the hallway, walking into the meeting, if you happen to cross paths at the gym, Starbucks, or a children's sports event.

When is small talk appropriate? Small talk has two important places in time: It should make an appearance in the minutes prior to or following any meeting or business function. This is your opportunity to tee yourself up for a successful business encounter. Again, use the small talk time to listen to the other person's voice. Do you hear nervousness? Confidence? Is this person pleased to see you or overly anxious? Does the person seem reserved, tentative? Bored or arrogant? These are all important clues that will help you assess and ultimately adjust your behavioral style in order to grow a strong relationship during the meeting. Use small talk time to gain and maintain the competitive advantage.

Another time small talk is appropriate is when you encounter a fellow business individual outside of a business environment. Perhaps you are meeting at a cocktail reception, sporting event, or a recreational facility. You want to connect with this person; however, it may not be the most suitable time to discuss business. For example, imagine yourself at a son's or daughter's sporting event when you notice one of the other parents is someone with whom you would like to connect. Certainly, it would not be appropriate to engage in business discussion here. However, making appropriate small talk can set you up for future business dealings. You can take full advantage of the social encounter by not saying a word about business. Never overstep business etiquette boundaries by crossing this line at social and business gatherings. By establishing a relationship and a connection, you lay the groundwork for the hands-on, hardcore business conversation that will take place at a later, more appropriate time and setting.

In some cultures, small talk is not simply a nicety; it is a prerequisite. In Asia, for example, no business is ever discussed during the first meeting. Rather, the first few meetings are all about building the relationship. They are devoted to sizing you up and skillfully, artfully conducting small talk. The initial meetings are in place so that the parties may get to know one another and begin to establish a trust from which to grow the relationship. Without this initial meeting and small talk, no further business is ever conducted. Far from being a small item, small talk is the critical first step. This is true in other high context cultures such as Asia and South America. Understanding the cultural requirements of small talk is integral to successfully conducting business in our global economy. Whatever your cultural background, you will need to be prepared to function in the environment where you hope to do business.

Why is small talk important? It is an icebreaker. It is also a means of obtaining information about the other person before business matters take over. This can be critically important. You may learn a valuable piece of information that you can use later. Perhaps you will recognize some common ground that can help develop the relationship. Small talk affords you the opportunity to discover common hobbies or similar or opposite interests, which will lead to a connection and help you establish the critical element of trust to help develop a strong business relationship.

The art of small talk can vary by location. Consider the following quick guide to small talk, organized by location.

In a client's office: Look around the room for conversation starters. Photographs of family or vacations are a good start. So are sports memorabilia and other personal items on the desk or shelves. Most people showcase their offices with items that reflect their character, hobbies, or interests, or have special meaning to them. Therefore, these are natural objects about which to demonstrate your genuine interest. By noticing these items and engaging in small talk about them, you demonstrate your desire to learn more about them. This will help build your own reputation and the relationship.

In your office: You may not want to have as many obvious items available for commentary. However, there is still plenty of opportunity for animated small talk when the visitor comes to you. It would be appropriate, for example, to ask a visitor about his journey to your location: How were the directions? How was the flight? Did you find your luggage? These are all perfectly acceptable small talk topics, and while they may not seem overly creative in theme, they will accomplish your objective nicely. You can use this brief discussion of last night's flight or this morning's traffic to gauge your visitor's demeanor and confidence level. Another possible topic: the weather. Although the weather may seem rather boilerplate, it is perfectly acceptable. Still, do not feel the need to avoid creativity in small talk. If you are a close observer, you may catch another opening. For example, I knew an individual who researched his prospective client and discovered that individual was a prominent alum of the college he too had attended. When he called on his prospective client, he made sure he wore the college logo cufflinks, which helped create a moment of positively charged small talk around their shared alma mater. Clearly, wearing the cuff links signaled the common bond of pride as well as an emotional connection.

At a networking event: In this arena, you will not have office décor to use as props. Therefore, you will need to be on your toes and very observant to make appropriate small talk. Items in and around the room such as murals, chandeliers, the grounds, the room decorations, or the building itself are all appropriate. Are the ice sculptures melting? Are the flower arrangements small talk worthy? Is the location of significance? These are all possibilities. Also, as you would visiting a client, see if you can spot an item on the individual, such as a lapel pin, that might initiate small talk effectively. Many people will deliberately wear some item specifically for this purpose, to help others more easily navigate the challenge of small talk as they seek to build a relationship.

Be careful when it comes to comments regarding another person's attire. Complimenting others is fine. However, it is not acceptable to comment or inquire about the item's expense, or to delve into details such as the designer or retailer. This might be misconstrued and considered fishing for financial status information, which is entirely inappropriate. However, noticing the individual wears a heart monitor on his wrist, suggesting he is a serious athlete is a great opening to talk about athletic prowess, accomplishments, pursuits, and so on.

At a social gathering: Even when we are not in a strictly business situation, the art of small talk is important and useful. The people we meet at parties, sports events, at the gym, or through our children's activities may one day be vital in our business lives. Executing appropriate and artful small talk in these situations is important. You never know—the person you chat with in line at the coffee shop may well be the linchpin in a business deal you have been hoping to pursue. Making small talk at the gym is fine, but be aware that some people like to work out in a "zone" without interruption. Offer an opening line and see how it goes. If the person picks up on the conversational thread, great. If not, smile, tuck this information away, and move on.

In social situations, it is important to read the signals during small talk to know your topics make colleagues comfortable. For example, it is perfectly acceptable to ask about and discuss what business the other individual is in. However, be sensitive. A person who has been laid off or is between positions may be reluctant. Be alert for a signal that suggests this topic is not a comfortable one.

One open-ended question I really like, which works well, can be used after you learn what business someone is in or which firm they represent. Ask the question: "How do you and how does your firm distinguish or differentiate yourselves in the marketplace?" This question reflects well on you and may well get them genuinely wondering about this critical business issue, in a good way. Try it!

Also, bear in mind that there is a distinct generational split when it comes to inquiring about one's profession. Members of the Baby Boom generation and younger will consider this question, for example, perfectly acceptable. Older individuals may take offense and think you are fishing for financial information if the question is worded, "What do you do for a living?" An important note, particularly if you are unemployed or in transition: Be especially prepared to discuss your situation as a matter of course, confidently and with ease during any social/business setting. Be prepared to ask for help; this is a networking opportunity! The person you meet may well end up being your critical connection to a new job. You never know.

Small Snags

Sometimes, despite the best preparation and intentions, things do not go as smoothly as you plan. Here are some common small talk challenges and potential solutions:

Challenge: The office you are visiting is sparsely decorated.

Solution: Not everyone has creative, conversational decor. Pick up on other clues and leverage them. Where is the office located? Is there a historic landmark nearby? There is something you can eye that will lend itself to a bit of small talk. Also, pay attention when you walk into the building and through the lobby and other public areas. Is there interesting art on the walls? Is the layout unique or interesting in any way? Are they expanding offices? Sometimes people don't help you by decorating their offices with interesting knickknacks, so you have to do some scanning on your own.

Challenge: The office sports quite a bit of décor, none of which you feel comfortable discussing.

Solution: Find a neutral way to comment. For example, the individual may have a photograph of himself shaking hands with a politician whom you do not admire. Or, there may be artwork you find offensive. An individual I know was horrified when she was escorted into a room where a Little Black Sambo statue was displayed. She found the statue racist and offensive and was quite thrown as to how to proceed. In a situation where you are confronted with material that offends you, you have two choices: You can ask about the item with interest, in an open-ended way, and listen to the response. It may be a very interesting story. Or, you may choose to ignore it and select another item on which to direct the conversation.

Challenge: You have engaged in a successful round of small talk with an individual you just met at a networking event, and now you need to disengage to work the rest of the room. Or, you have determined the person with whom you are speaking is of no interest or value. What to do? How does one disengage tactfully?

Solution: Say what you mean and mean what you say. Remember, you are endeavoring to build trust. Saying "I'll be right back" when you have no intention of returning is simply not true and will likely undo any progress you may have established. Instead, be straightforward and gracious: "Thank you, (name of person). I have so enjoyed meeting you and our time together. Will you excuse me please? There is someone on the other side of the room with whom I would like to speak. If we do not connect again before the end of the evening, perhaps we can catch up sometime within the next couple of weeks." Leave the suggestion open-ended. You have promised nothing. You have been gracious and are honoring your words. If possible, it would be thoughtful to introduce this person to another individual before you leave—the professional pass off.

Challenge: The person with whom you are making small talk has said or asked something inappropriate.

Solution: When possible, use humor. For example, if the person asks a question that is too personal, one which you are not comfortable answering, look for a clever way to deflect the question. Perhaps the person has asked how much you paid for your new home. Try "Oh, it's worth $10 million to me." Or the person has asked your age: "Sometimes I feel 100!" It is not unusual to have to confront these inappropriate questions. Many people are not well versed in the art and etiquette of deflecting and can be caught quite off guard answering and saying whatever comes to mind at the time. Be prepared to be gracious for both you and all concerned and make light of the question without feeling obligated to provide very personal information, which truly is none of their business.

Challenge: You are engaged in small talk and are interrupted.

Solution: Make good use of the extra preparation time. Instead of feeling awkward, use the time to look around the office for additional small talk topics. You may spot a squash racquet, a photograph from an exotic locale, or a dog-eared copy of a particular book. Do not assume your small talk time has been squandered. The savvy professional will use this time to enhance small talk conversation, thereby advancing the relationship, which is your goal.

Dangerous Topics

Some topics are simply poor choices for small talk. Consider the following examples.

Politics: Today's Red State/Blue State environment has become so polarized that the topic of politics can be quite a minefield. Best to leave it off the list of topics. If you are asked a political question, you can try to give an upbeat yet neutral answer and navigate the conversation onto a new subject. I knew a gentleman who told me he had gone to a meeting, fully prepared to invest with this firm. Upon learning during the course of making small talk conversation that these individuals were supporters of a political candidate whom this gentleman was diametrically and vehemently opposed, he made the firm decision not to invest with this company, based solely upon their political preference. The firm to this day has no idea why. Be careful.

Religion: Religion has always been one of the tried-and-true taboos for small talk. Religion inherently embodies too many pitfalls. You have no way of knowing when and how you might offend another individual when discussion topics pertaining to religion evolve, particularly today. Indeed, even two members of the same religion can have differing views, which risks misunderstanding and result in great misgivings. Anyone who has ever been involved in running a church or synagogue knows that even those of similar religious backgrounds can still have quite divergent views on key topics. Religion is a delicate subject that stirs great emotion, and rifts on the topic are challenging to repair, which is why avoiding the subject altogether during small talk discussion is advisable. For example, I have a photograph of myself with Cardinal Bernard Law. However, this photograph is not one which I display in my office area. Instead, I keep it in my home, where I entertain close friends and family. I keep other, less emotionally charged items in and around my office area where I receive business guests. This does not mean that I have misgivings about my photograph. Rather, consciously making the decision regarding where to display this demonstrates that I am aware of sensitive issues related to this photo and potential adverse reactions it may evoke. I choose not to showcase the photo in order to help ensure that my business guests are at ease. I display other items in my office that will foster "safe" small talk conversation.

Personal Issues: Topics considered overly personal include health, finance, and religion. While this is a good time to get to know the other individual, there are boundaries that need to be respected. This helps keep both parties in professional comfort mode and at ease. Remember, this is a time to build trust and the foundation of your business relationship. Too much "sharing" can completely sabotage your quest.

Safe Topics

Some topics are simply ready-made for small talk.

The weather: It affects us all. And it is endlessly interesting. Do not overlook the weather as an acceptable and rich topic for small talk. Certainly in recent years the weather has produced more than its fair share of news.

A good book: The smart and well-prepared person will attend an event or meeting prepared to discuss current events or a good, recent book. This is a sign of an intelligent, aware, curious individual, which will reflect well on you, especially if you can recommend a truly engaging read.

Transportation: This is another topic with which most all of us have direct experience. It is perfectly reasonable to ask an individual how he or she arrived at the location. It may spark an interesting story. Or you may learn a new shortcut in your well-traveled route. Because most business people travel, the ins and outs of the road warrior are often comfortable common ground. We all know how it is to be stuck in traffic, navigating crowded airports, managing our comings and goings. This is a natural connection.

Your surroundings: This can be anything from the actual room you are in to the new, historic, or restored building to the city itself.

Sports: Although sports can stir great passions, it is still safe, and safer than politics or religion for small talk conversation. Team sports are not the only option. Your colleague may participate in a sport. Look for clues such as a wristband, a sports watch, or anything in the office environment that might reveal, for example, an avid golfer, runner, or cyclist.

The other person: Little is more important or interesting to most people than themselves. If, by asking open-ended questions, you can get individuals to talk about themselves during your time together, you will find this to be enormously helpful. That person will likely leave the conversation feeling as though you were an extremely engaging individual and will remember the encounter as a positive experience. Conversation is an art, a skill. The key to making successful conversation is asking open-ended questions all about the other person and then engaging in active listening. Listen, listen, and listen some more. Respond by using facial expression, your eyes, and body language to communicate your response. Barbara Walters is a true icon and a woman I regard highly. She is an amazing woman who has built a tremendously successful career in the art of drawing people out and encouraging them to talk about themselves. Ms. Walters is frequently asked how she so successfully manages to get so many important, notably private people to open up to her and tell their stories. Ms. Walters has said, "Conversation skills are easy. One of the best ways to initiate a conversation is to ask questions. And what do people like to talk about more than anything in the world? Themselves!" Therefore, to be a great conversationalist, ask open-ended questions about the other person!

Suppose you are engaged in small talk and realize you are doing all the talking about yourself. Recognize this has worked from the other individual's perspective and that you have been artfully, successfully reeled in during this particular round. The other individual has successfully gotten you to share, however, you have learned nothing about them. If time permits, you may try to turn the conversation around by acknowledging this and saying something to the effect of "Oh, I have done all the talking. Tell me about you." Proceed directly to asking open-ended questions about them. Or you may simply have to accept this as a "miss" and try to do better next time. We all miss. It's okay. This is how we learn. Learn to recover, practice the art, and work harder during the next round.

Besides Talk

Finally, be aware that to be successful in the art of small talk is about much more than just words and talking. To be a savvy conversationalist, you must use your entire body: facial expression, eyes, posture, and stance. Be sure you make direct eye contact during conversation, which requires concentration. If you are at a networking event, you may want to scan the room for people you would like to meet. Resist that urge and focus all your attention, especially your eyes, on the person of the moment. Making that person feel important in that moment is your goal. By looking directly into that person's eyes, you demonstrate that you are giving him or her your full attention. Your time together is that much more special and memorable. This is a small nuance, but one which resonates with many people. Anyone who has ever met or observed President and Mrs. Clinton shake hands will attest to both their seemingly natural "technique" of lingering a bit for an extra second or two. Why? Making others feel as though they are really meeting "them." Making people feel very special, indeed. A great lesson from which we can all take a cue.

It is tremendously disheartening to speak with someone who is looking elsewhere. You will be well received when you make strong eye contact and make the other person feel as though she is the most important person, indeed, the only other person, in the room, which is your goal.

You can indicate your interest in other ways as well. Your body language speaks volumes about your interest and how you are feeling about yourself and the other person. When you sit at a desk or table, remember to be aware of how you are sitting: forward in your chair, with an invisible "V" between you and the back of the chair, which automatically encourages you to focus your attention forward to indicate your interest. Respect the temptation and resist the urge to lean back, appearing too relaxed, unprofessional, and disinterested. Keep arms in front of you, on the table; you are not about to draw your sword!

I remember meeting with a senior partner in a Boston law firm, seated at a small, round table in one of the conference rooms. I had my hands in my lap and noticed the attorney get up from his chair, come around the small desk and look directly down at where my hands were resting in my lap. My reflex reaction was to instantly place my hands on top of the desk, where he could view them. I did not get the account. Although I am not suggesting the sole reason was I had my hands in my lap, I am suggesting that I was not successful in developing trust.

Other aspects of sitting etiquette: Feet belong firmly planted on the floor (men and women), or, for women, sloped to the right or the left. Correct positioning suggests an air of professionalism, focus, and a show of respect toward your counterpart and to the conversation. Your body positioning tells others that you are an active participant and an active listener, which is as important as the final contract negotiations.

Finally, remember the importance of your voice in the conversation. Voice, tonal quality, inflections, and pace are all ways in which we can further demonstrate genuine interest in the other person. Be sure your questions and responses convey energy and enthusiasm. Americans tend to underestimate the importance of small talk in the business arena. Here in North America, we are all about business; time is money. We want to get down to the heart of the business meeting. While this is ambitious and admirable, the zealous, overly anxious individual may betray emotions through voice. It is important to give attention to your voice and make sure it conveys your intentions. Remember, small talk is the prelude. Conversation is the practice, all prior to the actual performance. It sets the tone.

When is small talk over? That depends. If you have called the meeting, it is your responsibility to call time for small talk and transition into business discussion. However, if you are the visitor, follow the lead of your host. While one person may be content with only a few lines of small talk, others may have different preferences. The entire first meeting may be devoted exclusively to small talk and not to non-business related topics. Again, this will vary among cultures and countries. Do your research so that you are prepared. It is wise, then, to be skilled in the art of small talk, which is always your biggest first challenge and opportunity.

Please remember: Small is big. Despite its name, small talk is critical to building a business relationship. Take it seriously.

SMALL TALK TIPS

- First, observe. Your small talk will be more effective if you take the time to look for the best possible icebreaker.
- Stay safe. Avoid emotionally charged topics such as politics and religion.
- Ask open-ended questions. This encourages the other person to open up and share, giving you even more information.
- Make strong eye contact, a key indicator of your interest and respect.
- Be aware of your body language revealing how you really feel.

4

Networking

It is just after work and you are on your way to an event that you believe will be a major networking opportunity. You are dressed appropriately, have brought plenty of business cards, and have arrived on time; however, you have failed to take one crucial preparation step before you left to help ensure your evening's success. What is it? You did not eat. While there will no doubt be food in abundance at this event, remember, you are not there to eat. You are there to work, artfully network, and contribute. You are there because you and others can benefit from and contribute to this event. Therefore, be certain your actions are consistent and communicate this message. Making a beeline for the buffet only communicates that you are hungry and less interested in meeting and speaking with others.

Etiquette is a crucial and often overlooked aspect of networking. Many people consider themselves quite good at working a room. When in fact, they are often more adept at enjoying a room than they are at advancing their own careers. Networking is a complicated and delicate dance. Utilizing proper etiquette will have a dramatic impact on how well you move.

A networking event is a gift, an opportunity to present one's self in a positive light to colleagues, superiors, industry leaders, and potential clients. Networking is an invitation to make yourself known to those you might not otherwise have the opportunity to meet face to face and to shake a warm hand, look into their eyes, and make a great impression. Only the shortsighted in business today do not recognize the value a networking opportunity presents. Most understand that success in business is a combination of intelligence, luck, chance encounters, and connections. Networking is your opportunity to enable a chance encounter to help build critical connections and relationships. Networking can happen anywhere. Certainly, events such as dinners, association meetings, and cocktail parties are obvious networking opportunities. However, the savvy professional is always on the lookout for a network opening that can occur at a wedding, a support group meeting, or a youth sports event. Appropriate protocol and behavioral standards are critical to making the most of any networking opportunity. Operating within acceptable modes of behavior puts you in good graces with your networking target. The respectful, professional behavior and genuine demeanor you exude reflects well on you and puts anyone you meet at case.

Try not to regard networking as a chore, but rather as a wonderful gift, an opportunity in place to help further yourself and advance your career. How many of us have finished the day aware that we have a networking event penciled in on the calendar, and migrated toward a colleague, sighing, "Okay, let's go, just put in an appearance. Fifteen minutes and we are out of there"? However common, please know this attitude and approach are utterly self-sabotaging. While many do not enjoy networking, please be mindful that networking presents a tremendous opportunity, literally presented to us on a platter, to meet those we would not otherwise have the opportunity to meet and to be seen in a favorable light. The savvy professional will use this opportunity to advance their career. Advancing one's career does not happen in "15 minutes and we're out of here." Networking is our lifeline to connections, and it is an art, a methodology that mandates preparation, approach, discovery, savoir faire, and follow-up.

There are three separate and distinct phases involved in networking: before, during, and after. There are rules and etiquette in place to help us successfully navigate what can be, for many, an intimidating process. The better you are at executing each phase, the more you will benefit from the event itself, further distinguish yourself in business, and advance your career.

Before the Event

Preparation is key to any successful networking event. Your first move should be to obtain the list of attendees. This is not difficult to do. Ask the person who either coordinated the event or the person to whom you responded. It is not unusual these days to make this request; therefore, this should not present a challenge. Should you be asked why, be straightforward in your reply: "I am very much looking forward to contributing to a successful event and want to be as prepared as possible."

Once you obtain the guest list, review this on several levels. First, read, review, and practice pronouncing names. There is absolutely nothing we as people enjoy more than hearing the sound of our names pronounced properly, particularly those with challenging first or last names. This is a small yet powerful way to convey respect and demonstrate your time, attention, and focus on details. This enhances your image. What else does this person take the time and make the effort to learn about, practice, master, and execute? I want to do business with this individual. This is an overt show of respect that also distinguishes you.

I knew a bank senior vice president who would spend 20 to 30 minutes prior to each and every banking and business event the bank hosted reading, reviewing, and practicing pronouncing names. The look on people's faces following the formal introduction, once they heard him say their name fluidly, as if he had known it and them forever, was powerful and spoke precious volumes. The message was clear: This person was a professional who was clear, focused, and present. He was an individual with whom to be reckoned. Translation: I want to do business with him, because if he is this attentive to a small detail such as how to properly pronounce my name simply to prepare for a networking event, what else does this individual devote time, attention, focus, and detail? How much more could we expect from him in regular and ongoing business dealings? Bottom-line impression: I have confidence in this individual. I want to do business with this person.

Second, review the guest list in order to do further diligence and preparation. Learn the participants, their current business focus and anticipated activities. This will provide you with valuable information and give you something specific to ask about, demonstrating that you are aware of their challenges, platform, ambitions, and even perhaps their firm's vision or mission statement. The effort you put forth in this regard will surely be acknowledged. Very few people actually do this step. Here is yet another terrific opportunity!

Third, look for connections and business affiliations. Look for ways that you can both benefit from and contribute by understanding that big-time connections can be made. Do some research on the companies or individuals you see on the list. This can be invaluable when you meet at the event and need to make intelligent small talk. A little research ahead of time can give you the air of a pro. I once met an individual at an event who, when he shook my hand, told me his name, his title, and the business he was in. Because I had done some research ahead of time, I was able to respond, "I am very pleased to meet you. I know your company and am aware that your nearest competitor is XYZ Corp. I am curious to know, how do you differentiate yourself in the marketplace?" The individual was immediately engaged and proceeded to respond in a very proud, deliberate, yet pensive manner in conversation together with me. A few quick clicks on the Internet and I was able to successfully launch a timely connection.

Another useful tool that may require some research: Be prepared with some relevant, current discussion topics. Can you talk intelligently about a recent event in the news? Or recommend a good book? Discuss a current artist or author? This may take a bit of pre-event research; however, it will help you impressively distinguish yourself.

Finally, set priorities. Seek out those individuals on the list you know you want to meet. Perhaps there is someone you have been unable to reach on the telephone. Or, there is a more senior executive at your own firm you would like to meet and would like to have know you. Maybe there is a person in another department you might benefit from knowing better. Networking events are timely opportunities. I encourage you to take advantage of the opportunity and seize the moment. Remember you are not the only one who may be thinking "15 minutes and I am out of here." Therefore, you will want to keep your priority list in the forefront of your mind and use your time wisely so your clock does not run out.

In addition to reviewing the guest list, you should work up your own tag line for the event. What is a tag line? A tag line is the one-sentence introduction you deliver when meeting someone. This may change from venue to venue, depending on your audience. Example: "Hello. My name is Judith Bowman. I am a principal with Protocol Consultants International and, among other things, I happen to be a syndicated columnist. I write!" Be sure to say "hello" and not "hi." Use first and last name, title and company affiliation—this is a professional event, not a social event. People need to know and identify you with your business, affiliation, and what you do. It is not only about how they can help you, but how you can help them; position yourself as a resource. Remember to help make the association for others to remember your name. Do your best to make your tag line brief, clear, and engaging.

On the Day of the Event

Dress professionally. Dark colors work best for men and women. White, off-white, or khaki colors are generally only appropriate in warm weather and tropical climates. Choose a suit with large pockets, one for incoming and one for outgoing business cards. Do not place your own cards any place where it would be difficult to retrieve when asked or offered, such as your purse or a wallet. Have business cards easily accessible.

Eat something prior to the event. This bears repeating. You are not invited anywhere because someone thinks you need to be fed. You are invited because someone wants to thank you for your business, or because someone believes you can contribute to the event's success. People who enter a networking event and make a beeline for the buffet table have missed the opportunity and the point of gathering.

Before you enter the event, make a stop in the rest room. Do a thorough mirror check for overall appearance: hair, teeth, buttons, zippers, makeup, ties. Pop a breath mint. And finally, wash your hands with warm water and soap and dry thoroughly. This will help you avoid the dreaded "clammy handshake" once the real work of networking has begun.

Another pre-entry check point is the name badge table. Be sure your name badge is fixed on your right shoulder. This puts it in the line of sight for anyone shaking your hand. Having the name badge in clear view will also help others to remember your name, a key goal we should all endeavor to embrace during any networking event. Refrain from placing your name badge on your belt buckle, for example, forcing the other individual to look down to greet you by name. Make it easy for fellow colleagues to clearly view your name, first and last, and affiliation if appropriate, to better facilitate conversation and introductions. As with any point of etiquette, doing so will put others at ease, which will reflect well on you.

Once you have finished with all your pre-event preparation, you are ready to make your entrance. And yes, it is an entrance, and those already in the room will notice you as you enter. Therefore, enter with an eye towards making a good impression. Be sure you have a pleasant, approachable expression on your face as you go in. Sometimes we are not always aware of what our own natural expression may be. If you are not sure, ask someone whom you trust to tell you the truth. Do you appear approachable?

I received a call once from a woman who told me her husband had just received a promotion to a top-level position at a Fortune 3 firm. She first asked for help for herself, so that she would have top-flight skills in her role as a corporate spouse. However, when I met the couple, I immediately saw who my true client would be. I met the couple at the door and said: "Congratulations, Mr. X! What would you like to work on today?" To which he replied, "Well, I don't know why people feel they can't relate to me." This was said with a completely expressionless face, monotone voice, and dead eyes. Clearly, the man was brilliant, or he certainly would not have achieved the position he had earned. However, he simply needed to be made aware of the way in which he was being perceived. All he had to do was put some energy into projecting his voice, infuse tonal quality, inject "life," use his warm eyes, some facial expression, stand up straight, and exude a positive attitude, confidence!

Role play and practice in front of a mirror. This really can help, because we are not always aware of our own natural facial expression and the ways in which we are perceived by others.

Now, with all your preparation and practice behind you, you are ready to begin. As you enter the room, know that most people watch the entrance to see who is arriving. Use this to your advantage. Step in and step aside. Pause 15 seconds and scan the room. Allow your eyes to make dead-on eye contact with others. Then, begin to work the room. Walk slowly, confidently, through the room. Remember, attitude is everything! Your mind-set says this is your event, your room. The aura you exude will permeate the room as you confidently wend your way through.

Networking etiquette is about meeting people you would not normally have the opportunity to meet, affording you the great privilege of putting them at ease in order to draw them out and develop a personal rapport. Understand the rules regarding who, when, and how to approach. For example, is it acceptable to approach two individuals engaged in conversation? What about those standing alone, or groups of three or more? Generally speaking, it is not wise to step in on a couple. Two individuals involved in conversation should not be interrupted. That said, how many times have you been "stuck" with someone whom you have determined is of absolutely no value to you and your purposes? How do you tactfully deal with the "clingers-on"? Do be sensitive to this possibility as you notice that two appear to be deeply engaged and walk past slowly. Make eye contact. Look for an opening. Look for the nonverbal signals that would invite you to join in. Singles standing alone will most likely welcome your approach. In a group of three, often there is an "odd man out" and your approach will be welcomed.

When you meet someone, be the first to extend your hand to offer a firm handshake and lean in with a warm, inviting smile. There are no gender rules regarding who can or should offer a hand first. Indeed, you should strive to be the first to offer a handshake. The person who initiates the handshake automatically acquires the power position, has the opportunity to control the introduction, and facilitate conversation, a skill that we should consistently strive for in every business setting. Be prepared to shake a lot of hands and exchange many business cards at networking events. Be goal-oriented and at the ready. When you extend your hand, do so with your thumb up, lean in, exude confidence and be a man/woman well-met. Shake hands like you want to meet this person, have them know who you are, and be remembered in a most positive way.

If you are holding a glass, be sure this is in your left hand so that your right one is available for handshakes, not wet and clammy from the glass's condensation. What to do when holding your glass in one hand and your hors d'oeuvres plate in the other and suddenly, someone wants to introduce you? Should you try to balance the two? Put one or the other down quickly for the handshake? The answer is never, ever put yourself in that position to begin with. Remember, you are not there to eat. You are not even there to drink. If you feel it is appropriate, consider something that appears festive but is not alcoholic, such as cranberry juice with lime. Another option: a diluted glass of wine. It is wise to limit your intake of alcohol at networking events. Remember, this is work, not a party, and there are many who became loose-lipped after a cocktail or two and who have paid the ultimate price.

Contribute to the event's success. You were invited because someone thought you would contribute, therefore, do not let your host down. Be open and approachable. Project energy and enthusiasm in your demeanor and conversation. Whenever possible, use the word "help." For example, "Perhaps I can be of help," or "I'd like to help you," or "How can I help you?" We as human beings respond to the word "help," which is part of our nature. Remember to use this phrasing, as it is an opportunity to get involved and do business within the context of an appropriate networking venue. Often, using the word "help" in this way enables others to feel less guarded and more open to engage.

Should you stand or sit? Standing allows you the best possible opportunity to move, maneuver, and network. Sitting limits your options and may convey the misperception of disinterest, even arrogance. However, should your conversation counterpart opts to sit, by all means, retire to a venue more conducive to conversation, to reinforce and encourage your colleague's comfort zone, to mirror behavior, and to make the connection. This will also open up the one and only time it would be completely appropriate for you to eat at a networking event. Should your colleague opt to partake in the food and sit down at one of the cabaret tables, this is your signal to follow suit. Select easy-to-eat "toothpick" foods. Avoid anything with sauces or that is difficult to dissect. You will not make a favorable impression if a clam shell flies across the table or crumbs land on your lapel.

As a general rule, invest three to five minutes with one person before moving on. However, be very careful when disengaging. Be clear and be honest about what you're doing. Remember, you are there to earn trust and grow a relationship. Never say, "I'll be right back," when you do not intend to return. Say what you mean and mean what you say. Protocol suggests being tactful and direct: "I have so enjoyed speaking with you. Thank you for your time. There is someone I need to speak with on the other side of the room. If we do not reconnect this evening, perhaps we can catch up within the next few weeks." This leaves the options, open-ended, promising nothing, saying what you mean, and meaning what you say. Then, it would be gracious to introduce this person to another guest, so as not to leave the individual feeling abandoned.

Question: Should you approach an individual who outranks you? For example, a senior executive at your company or an industry luminary?

Answer: Absolutely. One of the marvelous benefits of a networking event is that it affords you the opportunity to meet those individuals outside your regular circle of colleagues, competitors, and contacts. Be confident you make a great first impression before you make your move. Are you prepared to make relevant small talk? Are you armed with information and telling or compelling questions, specifically regarding their firm, their responsibilities, and their business? Be careful here, however, regarding becoming entrenched in business talk at this opportunity. Can you offer congratulations regarding their firm's growth or reaching a critical milestone? Can you succinctly describe your connection to this event and the host company? Particularly if you are speaking with a senior member of your own firm, be prepared with a relevant comment regarding the company and how honored you are to be a part of the team.

Be sure to say thank you for the opportunity to help contribute to achieve company goals and objectives. The simple words "please," "thank you," "I am sorry," and "excuse me" are not said often enough! And others rarely tire of hearing those basic, simple words, particularly in high context cultures.

When it comes time to exchanging business cards always ask, "May I offer you my card?" or "May I ask you for your card?" What is key here is *always ask*. Never assume anyone wants your business card. I have actually had people say to me, after I have asked, "No, Judy. Actually, if you would like to send me something back at the office, fine. However, I really do not want to collect a lot of cards here tonight." People will tell you! Always ask. While it may seem obvious that business card exchange will take place, asking shows respect and demonstrates that you make no assumptions. After receiving another person's business card, place this someplace respectful, such as one of your predesignated front pockets or your inside breast pocket. If you want to make notes on the card itself, do so later, not in view of the individual. You are quite literally defacing their "life." When you think about it, the size of a business card is small. Taking or making notes on the back of the small business card, if they ask you to do this, suggests the information regarding their firm is small and insignificant.

One important note about meeting a high-ranking executive: Never ask a very senior executive for his business card. Protocol suggests that top-level leaders exchange business cards only among their peers, which is accepted practice among the upper echelons of business leaders. The inference is you know how to find that individual and follow-up after the event. Should a very senior executive ask for your card, you should consider this a great compliment.

Make it your goal to meet as many people and shake as many hands as possible throughout the course of the event. Keep in mind that people do notice one another at events and that individuals diligently, enthusiastically working the room will absolutely be seen as ambitious, focused, and professional, while the person lounging by the bar or scarfing food at the buffet table will be seen as, at best, hungry, disinterested, and unprofessional. I was once at an event where I worked the room well and thoroughly, and as I left, was approached by a senior executive who had also been in the room. "Who are you?" he asked me. "I watched you work that room and I decided I needed to meet you. I'd like to hire you to do what you just did for me." This drove home to me a premise I shall always remember: At any event, you are on the business stage and others are evaluating you, your behavior, your demeanor, attitude, and professionalism.

After the Event

Post-event activities are critical to complete all the efforts invested heretofore. The way in which you depart is also an art and a process that, again, presents many opportunities for you to shine. Exiting anything, from a large event to a small dinner party, is an art. When you demonstrate graciousness, appropriate etiquette, and finesse in your departure, you walk away knowing that your final impression, the note on which you exited, was polished, precise, professional, and served your purposes of helping set you apart.

When you are ready to leave, your first responsibility is to make others feel good that they made the effort to attend and speak with you. Thank people for their time and for coming. Find and thank your host for inviting you.

In most cases, when you think about it, the real talk of networking, indeed, the most substantive conversations, take place as individuals leave an event. Real talk can happen in the coat-check line, outside the building, or even in the parking lot. The final moments can be the most important. They are often when conversations are more relaxed, less guarded. It is not a good idea to trail a key connection out to the parking lot. However, when the opportunity presents itself, make the effort to walk out with them and catch a few minutes of candid post real talk; this could be the most powerful networking moment of the evening. If you are hosting the event, be sure to escort guests out, just as you would a guest in your home.

As you leave the event, check the business cards you have collected and, privately, make notes as needed on the back. Putting this off will compromise your memory of important details, which will serve to help you with critical follow-up. Further, be discreet in doing so. Be sure to follow up with those you met the next day or as soon as possible after the event.

You may be tempted to follow up only with individuals who could be useful to you now, or perhaps in the near term. Please be reminded that this is a mistake and, not surprisingly, poor etiquette. Follow up with everyone you met, thanking them for their time, expressing an interest in remaining in contact, letting the individual know that you valued your time together. This demonstration of high-end business courtesy goes a long way towards making a positive lasting impression and distinguishing you in a most favorable way. Why bother if you don't need the individual now? Good networks are collections in constant need of care and attention. A strong networker knows to keep connections at all times, not simply as an emergency source when something goes wrong. Displaying proper etiquette and proactive people skills, particularly when you do not currently need a favor, showcases you as a polished example of an individual who is self-assured. The other person will more likely have a positive memory of you in future business dealings.

What format for follow-up? E-mail is fine for a brief networking follow-up, particularly in dealing with an "e-minded" or "e-culture" company. E-mail is an efficient, proactive means of communications in business today and it is accepted commonplace business practice. While I would never recommend an e-mail thank you or follow-up alone, another, more personal gesture, the actual handwritten note, is never wrong and will certainly propel and distinguish you from your competitors. Considering the person you met last night also met 20 other people, this can only work to your advantage. Please note: The brief, handwritten note on your personal, quality stationery, (blue ink is for social correspondence, black ink for business) with a stamp versus a postage meter, makes a powerful, personal, lasting statement.

It is also appropriate to follow up via telephone, particularly if you were not able to carry on a three- to five-minute conversation at the event. I was recently at an awards ceremony and was seated at table of 10. I was not able to speak to everyone; however, we all did exchange business cards perfunctorily. The next day, I followed up by phone with each person, and with each I asked, "Please tell me about your expertise." One individual with whom I spoke was somewhat skeptical and not sure what I might be up to. He was in the headhunting business. So I said, "I can sense you are uncomfortable and want to let you know I am just trying to be efficient here. I do a lot of networking, attend many events, and I am trying to make them worthwhile for everyone. You never know who I may run into who might be able to utilize your senses. I need to better understand what it is you do and who you are looking for so that, should I come across a candidate who fits your profile, I can more efficiently direct them. I would like to be able to help you." This completely changed his mind-set. When you let people know you would like to help them, this gets their attention and makes them more willing to connect and do business with you. Remember, when following up, offer to help the other person. Networking is a two-way street.

 HOW TO RECOVER IF...

...you realize you have spent half the networking event chatting with friends.

Clustering is a common faux pas at networking events. You are there to network; to meet, greet, and make new contacts; and provide introductions. Should you find you have become part of a cluster, be a leader and suggest you all move out onto the floor and circulate, or simply excuse yourself and work the room.

NETWORKING TIPS

- Eat first. You are not there to eat.
- Drink sparingly, if at all.
- Approach singles and groups. They are most likely to be open to your advance.
- Maintain an approachable facial expression. Practice in the mirror or with a trusted friend if you are not sure how your natural expression looks to others.
- Shake a lot of hands: thumb up, lean in.
- Prepare a tag line: name, rank, and business affiliation.
- Take your time; do not rush. Take advantage of this 15 minutes opportunity.
- Concentrate now, take notes later away from others' purview.
- Follow up via e-mail, personal note, and/or telephone, even with those you do not believe can help you now.
- Offer to help others. You are there to benefit as well as contribute.

5

Telephone Skills

You have placed a call to a key customer, engaged in some small talk, and worked your way through your list of business issues. Whose responsibility is it to wrap up the conversation and bring it to a conclusion? Answer: Yours. The rule is: Whoever initiates the call is responsible for bringing it to a conclusion.

The telephone is a staple in the American home and workplace. We all know how to use one. Ironically, very few people are skilled regarding the most effective use of the telephone. When it comes to business, the inanimate telephone has its own set of skills and rules and most people in business need to be reminded. Many a businessperson spends sleepless nights worrying about business issues they cannot control. Most could improve their navigation skills, and, their night's sleep with small, focused attention to the critical elements of telephone skills and techniques. Although technically the telephone is a piece of business machinery, telephone usage in the business arena is an art, one that has often been overlooked and misused. Efficient use of the telephone in business should be repeated. It is a new area of productivity unto itself, waiting to be tapped.

The key to stellar telephone etiquette is not a question of manners, pleasantries, or niceties. Rather, it is understanding the technology and your goals as a business professional. A telephone, after all, has no life, no feelings, and no emotions; you cannot sense its mood, shake its hand, or ask for its help. It is a cold object that literally stands between you and your customer. Your challenge is to manage this object so that rather than a barrier, it is an efficient vehicle to help facilitate your purposes, goals and objectives. The first step in addressing the telephone challenge is to focus on overcoming the physical presence of the telephone as a thing: an obstacle. For all its marketing hype, the telephone does not create connections; people do. In business, the telephone is a hurdle. Envision yourself as a mountain climber surveying, considering, and scaling the landscape obstacles and possible setbacks that lie before you. Place the focus on the call as a means to help achieve your ultimate goal: personal connection, interpersonal communication.

How to Make the Most of the Telephone

Preparation

Before you dial, consider the telephone call as you would a presentation. You would never dream of going into a presentation unprepared. This would be a form of self-sabotage as it would be to enter into and participate in a conference or meeting "winging it." Certainly preparation for any presentation involves outlining an agenda and time frame, researching facts, and having a list of anticipated objections and ways in which you plan to counter those objections. Your tools include small talk and personal topics of discussion to have at the ready. Marshal your best possible energy and enthusiasm before placing the call. This is critical. If you don't have it, do not place the call. Rehearse and hone your pitch to your own personal best delivery status. You have limited time to have their attention. Make the most of it. Use hardworking, efficient words and selective word tracks. Be consistent with those the other person uses, in order to better relate.

You should dedicate time, effort and, pre-planning before you place your telephone calls. The telephone call is simply another form of presentation, one that is actually more challenging and requires more, not less, prep work. To prepare, do your research. Who are you calling? What is your goal in this call? Who might you encounter on the other end of the phone, however inadvertently? Be prepared! Do you know all their names, areas of responsibility, something personal to ask about or mention in conversation, if appropriate? What are some obstacles that may arise along the way and how will you address and deal with them?

Before placing any telephone call it is wise to have a tag line prepared: a quick one-sentence overview that speaks to who you are and what you want. This shows respect for the other person's time, and your efforts and efficiency in getting to the point of your call will, no doubt, be appreciated. Time is money. You are present in the moment and prepared to do business.

Preparing what to say is only one step in the pre-dialing process. Make sure you have all your key tools within reach. Will you need to refer to any documents or back-up information, or even need a glass of water, during the course of the call? Be sure they are all within arm's reach.

Prepare your office setting for the call. Close your door or position yourself in your area as closed. Access call-forwarding and voice-mail options. Notify others, if appropriate, that you will be on a call and ask them to hold off any interruptions. Be sure all your technology is set in such a way that you will not be disturbed. Resist the temptation. Close your e-mail; you can check it later. There is nothing more off-putting than realizing someone on the other end of the phone is checking his or her e-mail. Also, turn your cell phone ring off and be sure your call-waiting function is muted. The person you call should be made to feel as though she has your full attention. Remember your goal: make the other person feel as if she is the most important person to you, your only client. Do not let other people or technology interfere with that goal.

Finally, check your own energy level. It is critical to inject and infuse energy into your telephone presentation. Human nature, in general, is drawn toward positive energy. Is your voice ready for the workout? Is it prepared to convey energy, enthusiasm, and professionalism? Are you mentally and physically ready to focus on tone, diction, and delivery? If you are dragging and not in energy mode, you might risk being a total turnoff. Take a break. Take a walk, stretch, do anything you must to get your blood moving and your energy up for the call. Just as with a presentation, go into the telephone call with engines revving. There is no warm-up lap in a telephone call. You typically have only seconds to hit your mark.

Once you begin to dial, be prepared for whatever might happen on the other end of the call. You may be successful in reaching your intended target immediately. If so, terrific. You are good to go. However, more often than not, you will encounter two common interim glitches on the way: the gatekeeper and voice mail. We will address how to handle both.

First, the gatekeeper. There are many successful sales professionals who will share tips on how to get past the gatekeeper. I once paid a fee to attend such a seminar. The seminar leader had us all pair off and role play. The "trick," he said, was to pretend the gatekeeper was your best friend. We were to use all our vocal skills to communicate with this person as though he or she were our closest personal buddy. So, the pitch we generated sounded something like this: "Hi, Anne, this is Judy. How are you girlfriend?" We were to treat the voice on the other end of the phone as though she were our friend for years.

I vehemently disagree with this tactic. There are no "tricks" and this tactic is deceiving and disingenuous. The person who answers that telephone is not your personal friend or buddy. That person is a professional with a job to do. It should not be your intention to trick that person or pretend to be someone you are not. Doing so is disingenuous and does not build trust. Your goal is to develop a business relationship based on trust and build the connection. This process may begin with the gatekeeper. Pretending to be chummy with the individual is a terrible idea. It starts off your business relationship with this organization with a deceptive practice, a lie. Instead, treat that individual with respect, dignity, and professionalism. That is the first step to building a business relationship bonded by trust between you and all members of that organization.

Say hello rather than hi. This is a nuance, yet it is professional and powerful. Use your full name and title: first and last, position, and company affiliation. Be prepared with your tag line including who you are and what you want. Please remember the gatekeeper is not your enemy nor are they an annoyance in your path. Rather, the gatekeeper is your first point of contact with the company; your first challenge and opportunity. If you hope to have a relationship based on trust, it starts at this moment, with this individual.

Suppose you get voice mail, which in this day and age is quite likely. Be sure to tap three key tools when leaving a voice mail message: preparation, brevity, and energy. You will have organized a quick one-sentence pitch stating your name, title, affiliation, purpose of your call, time and date if appropriate, and your telephone number, always repeated, stated slowly, without ending in a question mark. Also, inform them when you will or will not be available for a return telephone call unless this is lengthy or complicated, and when they can expect to hear from you again. Your voice is clear, concise, precise, punctuated, collected, and intelligent, and return telephone call worthy. Tap your energy and enthusiasm. Leaving a voice mail message requires a positive, upbeat, energetic tone. You have to push through not only the telephone line but the barrier of the answering machine. Those are two mechanical hurdles between you and your prospect.

Be sure to inject a professional demeanor that includes energy and enthusiasm, which is infectious, into the message. Remember, people are attracted to positive energy, enthusiasm. This is your best hope of getting a return telephone call.

How can you project your best telephone energy? There are several techniques that may help. Try using a mirror. In my first real sales position I sold booth space for a trade show company and worked almost exclusively in inside sales over the telephone. I did not have the benefit of a personal meeting to shake a warm hand or look into someone's eyes. Therefore, I had the challenge of introducing, questioning, presenting, countering objections, and closing virtually cold. I had to embrace the challenge of bringing a level of energy and warmth to my sales presentation. Our sales and marketing director gave us one tool: a 3 × 5 mirror, which he suggested we place at our stations. He further suggested that, as we dialed and made our calls, we look into the mirror and pretend our reflection was the other person at the opposite end of the telephone. "Smile," he urged. You can actually hear a smile through the wires. We were encouraged to use our facial muscles and expressions, and a smile, to communicate sincerity and enthusiasm. I found the mirror to be a great tool. By watching my own facial expression, I was more aware of the way in which I was projecting my own energy and enthusiasm level and, thereby, being received in the same manner. I did not have to remind myself to smile when I spoke; I could see a genuine smile, my own, right before my eyes. This mirror proved to be a valuable training tool, one which I find helps bring necessary luster to any telephone conversation.

Also, consider standing when you talk on the telephone. I also did this when I sold booth space. It was not always easy, given we worked in very small cubicles and used telephones versus wireless headsets. However, I did my best and found that standing helped me better project strength, passion, and power in my voice. I communicated more forcefully and with more energy. My body language was reflected in my vocal tone. Rather than sounding as though I might be comfortably reclining in an office chair, I believe I was perceived as credible, professional, prepared, and ready to bound off the telephone and right into my client's office.

The mirror and the decision to stand directly impacted my telephone skills and, ultimately, my closing ability. When I joined the company, I was assigned to the lowliest trade show, "House World Expo." It was a housewares trade show being sold in the traditionally slow summer months and not a very sexy show. I helped sell out the show in three months. Because of this, I was moved up to regional computer fairs and sold those out as well. Within a year, I was selling Comdex, the industry's most renowned trade show. Around the office, we used to joke that someone had to die in order to be promoted to the trades. No one left, and you had to earn the right to sell it because it was so lucrative. I had earned the right. I was 26 years old, and this was the first time I was able to see effort lead to reward, realizing that all you really had to do was develop a personal style, engage the other person, and be persistent. I was earning an excellent income simply by making telephone calls. Developing skills and telephone techniques can absolutely make the mechanical barrier of this inanimate object not only disappear, but actually work for you!

In addition to energy, the confidence and professionalism exuded in one's voice, choice of words and word tracks, and language are critical to one's success on the telephone. They do not just happen. You need to draft it, work it, try it, refine it, master and own it, all in order to be positively received and effective. I mentioned this earlier when I discussed the gatekeeper; however, this holds true with any telephone conversation. Use professional language at all times. This sounds simple; however, if you listen to anyone on the telephone today, you will hear a barrage of unprofessional sounding words and phrases. Here are a few:

"Hi."

"Hey dude"

"What's up?"

"Hold on a sec."

"Uh huh."

"Yeah."

"'Bye."

"See ya!"

"How ya doin'?"

These and other casual linguistic phrases should be stricken from your choice of professional telephone word usage and conversation. The telephone call is an opportunity to present yourself and your company in a professional light and build a relationship. Being perceived as a professional is not a nicety; it is a must.

Saying "hello" is a small thing; however, the nuance is powerful. Hello is the word of a professional, rather than the call of a buddy. Hello starts your conversation in a professional tone. Use your full name, first and last, and your title, being careful not to rush in the process. Take your time. Say your name with conviction and pride, because you want to be remembered positively. You want to leave a positive impression; therefore, speak clearly, distinctly, and with energy. Allow pride and confidence to carry into your voice and convey your most professional self.

In addition to mastering your own telephone skills, be sure to train anyone in your office regarding proper use of the telephone. Give direction on how to answer, how to take a message, how to screen calls, and how to ask who is calling. Those who contact your firm will be quick to judge your firm by the way this individual conducts himself and handles or mishandles these issues. The impact says simply one of two things: professional or unprofessional. This individual, the first person they encounter on the telephone, should exude professionalism, energy, efficiency, warmth, and caring, because this will color and create callers' first impression of you, your brand, and your firm. Confidence, precision, and genuineness will also be noted and be part of the overall critical first impression of you and your firm.

Be sure to offer not just suggestions, but precise language and actual telephone skills training to staff.

We all know how a telephone works. However, making a telephone work for you as part of the business process requires skill, practice, technique, precision, and finesse. Be certain that you learn these skills, model them for your employees, and provide proper training for all to strive for excellence in this area. Employers today provide training on new software and other new technologies. Remember, the telephone is a device used everyday in virtually every business. What could be more important to master?

Special Situations

Today, the telephone is more than just a device on the desk. It is important to master and implement the necessary skills of its varied uses. The telephone is far more accessible and complex than it was just five years ago. I will now address just a few special situations that require more specific knowledge and attention.

Call waiting: The person responsible for this invention clearly never made a business call. The concept of call waiting, where one person is left hanging while you check and see if someone else more important is on another line, is a terrible concept for business. It is as if the cashier helping you were to check with others in line to see if someone else would like help first. How does that make you, "next in line," feel? Not good, certainly, and not at all as though you are the most important, most valued customer. Remember, this is your goal.

Please keep this in mind when using call waiting in business. There are many ways call waiting can undermine your attempts to establish the connection and build trust. Resist the urge to have called waiting interrupt your one-on-one calls. If you cannot disable or ignore the function, be prepared to handle call waiting in a correct, efficient manner. If you have call waiting and you know you are expecting a call that may interrupt, alert the other person in advance. Say, "I want to alert you to the fact that I am expecting a call." No need to explain from whom, where, or why. "Should this come in while we are on the line, I hope you will not mind if I take this call." This conveys respect to the person with whom you are currently speaking, and also lets them know that they remain your number one priority. Most will respond positively. While no one likes to be interrupted, it is courteous and respectful to be forewarned and asked permission. This should, however, be the exception. To interrupt one call to take another via call waiting does not enhance the relationship. Accessing call waiting, particularly without alerting and asking permission, suggests to the first individual that he or she is not your first priority.

Speakerphone: This is another form of high technology that should be treated with respect and used appropriately. Whether used one on one or in a conference call, it is critical that you display proper speakerphone etiquette. These devices can help or severely hinder a relationship, depending on your use of them. At the start of any one-on-one call, always ask permission to use the speakerphones, out of respect. Using speakerphones without asking is rude and disrespectful and will surely not help promote your business goals and objectives.

At the start of a call involving speakerphones and multiple participants, one person should be in charge of introducing the participants, rather than having each player say his or her name and title. As each is introduced, that individual should extend a greeting in order to help other participants associate a voice to the name.

Once the call is underway, it may be necessary to repeat your name and the capacity in which you function as you speak for the first time. This, once again, is a courtesy to other participants who are endeavoring to make correct associations. Remember to speak slowly, loudly, and clearly, so that high technology devices help facilitate rather than hinder the conversation.

When participating in a speakerphone conference call, remember to make your words count: Be direct and succinct. Do not take up air space. If you have nothing significant to contribute, do resist the urge to hear the sound of your own voice, which is annoying in any ordinary meeting and doubly so if you are straining to follow the topic on a speakerphone.

Take notes, just as you would in any meeting. Begin note taking as early as during the introduction phase, because this may be invaluable to you later in the call should you need to ask follow-up questions. Addressing the specific individual on topic by name, without being reduced to asking again, or being vague, is powerful. This keeps you in constant control of the agenda. And, once again, hearing one's name commands instant attention. Use names whenever possible when endeavoring to make a point, get another's attention, and convey respect on speakerphones, on the telephone, at a networking event, or at a meeting. Doing so will demonstrate that you have and continue to pay considerable attention to the introductions and make the effort to know the correct associations, all of which will reflect well on you. If you can keep track of the multiple participants on a speakerphone conference call, what other challenging details do you take the time, go to the trouble, and make the effort to keep track of and pay attention to? Bottom line: I want to do business with you. Savvy business professionals appreciate that level of effort.

Cell phones: Remember when a telephone call was a private matter? Remember when telephone calls were handled inside the four walls of an office, a home, or at the very least, a telephone booth. Those were the old days. Today, the advent of cell phones suggests telephone conversations are held in public. Cell phone callers walk and talk in the street, their cars, public places, airports, the soccer field, public transportation, hallways, and stairwells. They may be personal; however, they are just as likely to be business calls, which suggests you must be savvy in the art of cell phone etiquette.

If you must make a business call on a cell phone, keep it brief with your voice low and professional. Shouting is not considered appropriate in business. Enough said. Should your party be unable to hear you well, simply find somewhere else where there is perhaps less background noise. Yelling and shouting will not enhance your professional image.

Remember, people around you may be listening. This is part of human nature. Plus, ironically, you may notice that the lower one's voice becomes in an effort to be discreet, the more finely tuned other's ears instinctively become. Beware and be aware! It is true that most of us try to ignore the cell phone conversations of others. However, if you are having a business conversation, be aware of your surroundings and the possibility that business information you are discussing may inadvertently be overheard and ultimately made public. Respect your own business and that of your client by keeping sensitive information private.

The number one rule regarding cell phone etiquette is this: As soon as you reach your destination, turn it off. Remember to silence your cell phone in any room or building where the ring might be unwelcome. A cell phone should never ring during a business meeting or lunch. If you feel the need to check your messages, excuse yourself and do so discreetly. If your cell ringer is on, avoid the many au courant ring tones now available. Your ring tones communicate your personal identify and your relationship with your phone: toy or tool? Have your cell phone and ring tone exhibit the same level of professionalism you strive for in all your other professional endeavors.

Finally, it is critical that whether from the telephone, after an event, or after meeting any client or potential client: make personal notes about any information you have learned (for example, they are planning a vacation in the Caribbean, their son—get his name and age—is trying out for the lacrosse team, an elderly aun is having an operation). Why? So that when next you speak, rather than launch into pitch, counter, close, you can refer to these notes and inquire about their vacation, whether their son made the team, or the health of their aunt. This is perhaps the single most important activity you can and shall engage in, in order to help build the foundation for a strong relationship and develop a personal rapport.

Again, once you have the relationship, everything else follows. Develop the relationship!

 HOW TO RECOVER IF...

...you are caught multitasking while on a telephone call.

Multitasking is what we do! Too often, however, we are tempted to multitask while on the telephone. Please know that keyboard clacking is audible. If you are guilty and caught, apologize. Say, "I am so sorry. My computer is right in front of me." Do not dwell on the faux pas. And then turn it off!

TELEPHONE TIPS

- Smile while talking. Smiling helps you project warmth and energy into your voice.

- Treat the gatekeeper as a professional. Tricks will only make you seem tricky. They will not build trust.

- Stand while talking—another way to ensure your voice is strong, energetic, and projects well.

- Use a mirror when making a telephone call. This will help you remember to smile and use other facial muscles to better project through the telephone wires.

- Whether you are the caller or the recipient of the call, focus on the conversation. Do not surf the Internet, check e-mail, or tidy up your desk while on a telephone call.

- When placing a call, do not ask the person, "Do you have a few minutes?" No one ever really has time for anything these days. Instead put a positive spin on the question. "I have caught you at a good time? Yes?"

- Use scripts carefully. It is wise to have your telephone pitch planned out, and it is critical to have word tracks in place to be certain you hit your key points. However, be wary of the way a scripted pitch can sound canned.

- Set up the next meeting. Regardless of how well your first call may go, you will want to set up a face-to-face meeting, or at least another call. Be prepared with concrete suggestions for the next encounter.

- Know who controls the call. If you have placed a call, it is your responsibility to control the agenda and bring the call to a conclusion.

- Use professional and grammatically correct language. There is nothing about a telephone conversation that suspends the rules of etiquette and protocol.

- Whenever you get voice mail, leave a succinct, clearly articulated message with only your key data points.

sure it is businesslike. Tell callers what they should do to ensure a call back.

● When using a cell phone for a business call, be aware of your surroundings. Use discretion when discussing business in a public place.

● Be careful that new telephone technologies such as call waiting, ring tones, and other gadgetry do not interfere with your goal of building business relationships.

6

E-mail

You have come to a stalemate while working on a business project and seek counsel from a coworker in another department. You use e-mail as a method of communicating, which is standard operating procedure in your firm. Several e-mails later, there is still no resolution in sight. What to do? After three volleys back and forth via e-mail on the same topic, protocol suggests you either pick up the telephone or pick yourself up and visit your colleague the old fashioned way (in person), or at the very least, on the telephone. The continued exchange of e-mail suggests the topic is too volatile or complex to be handled via virtual correspondence and requires the human factor.

E-mail and the Internet have both evolved as high technology innovations. When used and deployed properly they have high impact and are effective. Both have forever changed how business is conducted and transacted.

I remember that when I started my business, I used to purchase lists of select companies and their decision makers. I would personalize form letters and stay up until all hours of the night running off letters, stuffing envelopes, signing, sealing, and stamping. Then the Internet emerged, and my bulk mailings gave way to my Web page and calls started coming in to me, from all over the country, asking me about our programs and services! The Internet and e-mail have changed the way most business is conducted.

E-mail is fast, efficient, and economical, and it has become an increasingly ubiquitous form of communication that allows individuals the world over to communicate. Weeks or days once spent amidst circles and reams of endless paper—letters, faxes, telephone calls, and messages—have all but evaporated, thanks to e-mail's widespread use. E-mail and e-technology are perhaps the most high impact technological innovations in business communication since the telephone.

That said, our challenge remains to adapt the timeless traditional rules to high technology issues of today. E-mail comes with its own collection of challenges. Because e-mail is so rampant, it is also abused and widely misused. Like any good tool, the skill in using e-mail must be developed, refined, practiced, and mastered. E-mail needs to be respected and used wisely and efficiently. The savvy business professional will use this technology not only as a means to communicate, but also as a means of enhancing and improving business relationships. When wielded with skill, e-mail etiquette can be a powerful weapon in business.

Question: When should you use e-mail?

Answer: There are no absolutes here. Often, this depends on the client or individual with whom you are dealing. When forging a new business relationship always ask: "How do you prefer to communicate? Via e-mail or hard copy correspondence?" Your clients' preferences will be made known. Asking shows respect for them, their preferences, and their corporate culture, and demonstrates that you are assuming nothing during the relationship-building process, as you continue to endeavor to show respect and establish trust.

Even though most professionals today use e-mail, do not be surprised when asked for back-up hard copy of the same material in addition to the virtual exchange. Similarly, it would not be inappropriate for you to ask if they would like both. Because no doubt someone is curious to see, feel, and touch your actual product, business card, brochure, or presentation to judge and perhaps evaluate paper quality, printing, engraving, and other factors that reflect you and the firm you represent.

E-mail and Websites can be built and designed to look spectacular and have all the bells and whistles. However, I strongly maintain that you can tell more about individuals and their firm by their business card and brochure and the color and quality of paper stock, setup, and printing than by any technical wizardry on a Website. Do they use quality materials or not? Is the information set professionally or not? Their choice materials represents them and their firm.

Certain information can be exchanged via e-mail. However, more sensitive and confidential documents must be addressed either on the telephone, via fax, or in person. Please know there are no hard and fast rules for the use of e-mail in this regard. This is subjective and discretion is key. An important e-mail rule: Never write anything in an e-mail you would not be proud to read on the front page of a major newspaper. If the e-mail has even the most remote possibility of inflicting the slightest amount of damage should it be made public, do not send it.

When writing business e-mail correspondence, there are ways to make the process more efficient. Use a direct, concise subject line. The subject line suggests the first impression of you and your intent for corresponding. You are one finger stroke away from delete. Maintain a business focus. Do not rely solely on your e-mail address. Identify yourself to the recipient using a straightforward subject line. Business professionals click quickly through a full inbox and will decide, in the blink of an eye, whether to read or delete. A bizarre or in any way questionable subject line will typically get deleted or spammed. High-technology viruses and other technological issues are real. When we open a business e-mail it should be recognizable as business correspondence. Often, the only information we have to make this decision is the subject line. Avoid sending jokes, pass-alongs, chain e-mail, prayers, poems, and other nonbusiness content. Treat e-mail with respect and take its use seriously.

Before You Hit Send

Use a greeting and a salutation. While many professionals are comfortable with e-mail, this is still a very impersonal way to communicate. Try to soften and humanize e-mail by treating e-mail correspondence like a letter. Use a greeting such as "Dear," "Good Morning," or "Greetings." All are respectful and embracing. Make the effort to close with a salutation (anything other than "Best Regards.") "My Best Regards," "Warmest Regards," or "Very Sincerely" are appropriate, just as they would be in a traditional letter. I am partial to the salutation "Respectfully Yours" when closing a proposal letter or formal note of correspondence. I like it in these instances because we rarely see this and, when you truly mean it, this will help set you apart by using a unique, most respectful salutation.

Use spell check. There is no reason for typographical errors in e-mail correspondence. Every major software program has a spell-check program. Use it.

Spelling errors in an e-mail suggest to the recipient you did not even bother to spend a few extra seconds in a spell check. The perception: What else does this person skip? What about their attention to detail? Absolutely nothing positive will come from sending any correspondence containing misspelled words.

Keep it short. E-mails that extend beyond one screen are probably not best suited for the digital format unless it comes as an attachment, where it is implied this is a lengthy document. Remember that while e-mail is an efficient means of business communication, it is not the only one. Faxes and the traditional postal service are fine and quite acceptable ways to ensure that information is accurately transmitted. Overnight mail is perhaps a better way of letting the other person know you mean it. Formal proposals should typically be sent via overnight mail. Do not feel compelled to use e-mail if other methods might have more of an impact and be better suited to the nature and length of your document.

Use bullets. Many professionals prefer printing out e-mail in order to read and perhaps work on the content. Either way, be sure to make good use of page setup and format with respect to spacing, bullets, enumeration, and other display functions in order to depict a clear, professional presentation. Bullets will highlight key points and the use of numbers is efficient. Please be aware that certain numbers in certain countries are considered unlucky or offensive, and may even imply death. Therefore, use of the asterisk is professional and a good neutral alternative. Also, consider spacing between paragraphs. Skip lines for clarity.

Use proper grammar. To be sure, young professionals today have invented a new language and tend to use this in virtual communication. Please know the shorthand of text messaging and other fun new linguistic tricks with spelling or grammar are suited only to casual e-mail communication. This is not appropriate in business. Rest assured that few in the professional business arena will be inspired with a surge of trust if your e-mails contain comments such as "CUL8R."

When e-mail first emerged, I believe we were all sensitive to use of lowercase in the actual e-mail address. Often, e-mails were case sensitive, and we were required to follow that protocol. Now, case sensitivity is less common and we have the opportunity to use upper- and lowercase in the e-mail address in a positive, memorable way. Capitalize the first initial, including the first letter of the intended's first and last names, when typing the name in the address window. Even in a bare-bones communication method such as e-mail, this nuance can be used as a powerful tool to help you stand apart. While use of lowercase is somewhat generic, there is nothing incorrect about using lowercase letters in the address or body of an e-mail. Capitalizing first letters in an individual's name will allow you to convey an added measure of positive attention to detail and demonstrate your respect for this individual. This is a small gesture, to be certain; however, it is one that will help build your positive image as a professional, finely attuned to detail and correct business protocol, and demonstrate respect.

Once you have determined e-mail to be the appropriate means of customer contact, e-mail can be used in virtually every manner of communication and can be leveraged as a tool for a formal self and/or company introduction. Defer to a formal tone and demeanor. I encourage use of honorifics such as Mr., Ms., Dr., or Professor until otherwise directed. Even then, if you get to the point where you call someone by his first name privately, in professional business correspondence that may be copied or blind copied to whomever, defer to being conservative and address him using his honorific, should you weigh this to be appropriate.

E-mail introductions are more common in business today and most experienced business professionals will not be put off when approached via e-mail by an unknown individual. However, whenever possible, try to get and use the name of the mutually respected third party to help pave the way for your introduction. Then, when you send the e-mail correspondence, right up in line one use that person's name: "I am grateful to Jack Johnson for suggesting I contact you directly." Remember of course that e-mails are read quickly. Your challenge is to get your reader's attention at the onset or face the hard consequences of a quick delete. Therefore, the professional setup and presentation, writing style, and length are all worthy of your meticulous attention in order to earn trust and command respect.

E-mails are also used in already existing business relationships and are well suited to meeting follow-ups, confirmations, updates, and the like. However, even in an established business relationship, e-mail etiquette rules apply.

As always, use a clear, concise, easily understood subject line. Often, it makes sense to use a keyword such as the name of the project and date throughout the correspondence, which also makes it easy for busy professionals to keep track during the course of an ongoing project.

In the greeting and salutation, always assume the formal unless or until invited to do otherwise. Remember, you are earning trust. You need to earn the right to advance. When uncertain, always ask.

Conform to the style and culture of the company yet maintain your personal style. It is critical to maintain your own standards and level of professionalism. Remember, clients come to you as the consummate professional in your field. Your goal is to inspire trust and project professionalism. While a less formal company may be perfectly comfortable using first names in e-mail correspondence, do resist the temptation to get too cozy with anyone, particularly in e-mail correspondence. Even in the case of an already established business relationship, respect the time of your reader and be concise. Bullet important points for easy reading, skip lines, stay on a one-page frame, and avoid extraneous information.

Can e-mail be used for a thank-you note? Yes, although this depends quite a bit on the company culture. Some firms are all about e-culture and prefer e-mail and all other correspondence be sent electronically. Know who these companies are, those who prefer electronic correspondence and who leverage technology as their primary communication tool, and respond to them accordingly. In such companies, it is blatantly clear that it is appropriate to use e-mail to send a thank-you note. However, in a more formal corporate environment, an e-mail thank-you note might be interpreted as disrespectful. A handwritten thank-you note on quality stationery, in professional black ink (blue ink should be used for social correspondence), with the timeless, traditional postage stamp vs. postage meter, is the mark of respect and proper protocol.

That said, sending a quick e-mail thank-you note, together with a formal handwritten note on quality stationery, is never wrong, is always appreciated, and presents yet another opportunity to get you, your name, and your brand in front of your client once again. Do consider utilizing both mediums.

I remember traveling to New York to work with a firm formally known as one of the "Big Eight" accounting firms. Executives in our seminar included the firm's president and his wife. When I returned to Boston and my office the next day, I opened an e-mail from the president, thanking me for traveling to New York and letting me know how much he and his wife and his professionals appreciated the seminar. I was grateful and elated that this gentleman had taken the time and made the effort to send such a thoughtful note so quickly! However, it was an e-mail thank-you note. And so, for me to have handwritten a personal thank-you note on quality stationery, and sent this through the U.S. Postal Service after this individual e-mailed me his thank-you note, would have been inappropriate and possibly a snub. Instead, I pressed "reply" and responded in kind. I then thanked him for inviting me. I did, however, also take the opportunity to say thank you once again in the cover letter accompanying my invoice—connect and mirror. Responding in kind is appropriate in business in order to connect. Growing the relationship is always the goal.

Know your audience. Know their individual styles and preferences and adapt to them. When dealing with a more traditional firm, e-mail can still play a more significant role in the thank-you process. For example, after the meeting, return to your office and send a quick e-mail note. Remember, the longer you wait to send a note, the less impact the gesture holds. "Of course I will be sending a note; however, I could not resist the temptation, nor let the day escape, without sending you a brief note to thank you for taking the time to meet with me today" might be appropriate. In this way, e-mail serves to remind them of who you are yet again, leave another imprint of you and your brand. It also demonstrates your sincere appreciation for their efforts and time they took to meet with you. Time is money. They gave you a valuable gift: themselves. You acknowledge and show your appreciation by saying thank you to these individuals as soon as possible after meeting. At the same time, let them know you will be sending a traditional thank-you note as well. Then, when that note arrives by mail, you will have had yet another opportunity to brand yourself and your firm, making two positive impressions and distinguish yourself.

International E-mailing

When communicating with those from other countries, particularly Asia, be sensitive and assume a very formal tone as these countries are very ritualistic, most respectful in nature, and steeped in timeless traditions, customs, and protocol. A formal, almost ritualistic approach should be your modus operandi and your efforts in doing so will not go unnoticed.

When e-mailing associates in Asia, again, the use of asterisks in place of numbers is recommended. In some countries and within certain cultures, numbers are unlucky or otherwise undesirable. Use honorifics: always err on the side of formality and be conservative. Use official and formal greetings and salutations such as "Respectfully Yours."

Be aware of reversing the surname, particularly when communicating with those from Japan. That said, Japanese executives are very aware and respectful of American ways here in our culture, and know our surnames are not reversed. Therefore, out of respect for and in deference to our ways, they increasingly are automatically reversing their surnames for us! When in doubt, once again, always ask. Your honest efforts in endeavoring to utilize correct protocols will not go unnoticed and will be very much appreciated.

Avoid humor, jokes, certain gestures, and culture-specific words or phrases that might be misinterpreted. Your cross-cultural colleague may be proficient in English; however, it is wise to take precautions and avoid cultural colloquialisms that might create misunderstandings.

Respond promptly. This is true for all e-mail, but it is especially important when it comes to international correspondence. Parties are already dealing with constraints due to distance and time zones. Send a prompt reply if even to respectfully acknowledge receipt of the material. Let the individual know you are in receipt of and are working on your response. Project a specific time frame when they can expect your official reply, and honor it.

Common E-mail Pitfalls

Everyone makes faux pas and mistakes, particularly given the volume of e-mail we all must contend with every day. There are many opportunities to make mistakes in this very common, fast-paced medium. Following are some common e-mail errors to be aware of.

Assuming familiarity: Resist the urge to assume familiarity, especially early on in the relationship and particularly in any written form or document, because this can ricochet and damage the business relationship. Maintain respect and respect boundaries when communicating via e-mail.

Avoid joke telling: E-mail aside, humor can be challenging enough, one on one. Pass along e-mail jokes and cutsie "emoticons" should all be avoided. What is considered amusing or engaging by one may be insulting to another. Do not risk this in business.

Trusting the delete key: E-mail is forever. Should you e-mail anything unintentionally, do not assume pressing the "delete" key will save you. Access to old and even deleted e-mail is not impossible. Almost anyone, including government representatives, can retrieve any e-mails you thought were long gone. Even the most technically savvy are not immune. Microsoft founder Bill Gates found his e-mails detailing his plans to thwart rival technology companies came back to haunt him in court. Therefore, a good rule of thumb is never e-mail anything you would not be proud to read on the front of a major newspaper publication. In e-mail, there is no such thing as "confidentiality," regardless of what the obligatory legal blurb says at the bottom of the screen. I once received a forward from a friend in one firm who had somehow intercepted an e-mail that contained confidential information about me from their friend in another firm. It happens. Be careful. Information does get passed along. The only recourse is to be sure you never hit "send" without being completely confident your e-mail is entirely appropriate and discreet.

Sending large or unnecessary attachments: Attachments are both a boon and a bane to e-mail. While it is certainly convenient to send attached documents via e-mail, this can oftentimes present challenges. Large attachments can slow down or even crash a computer, and they can also be vehicles for viruses and other dangers to company technology.

I once asked a prospective new public relations firm for a proposal, which they sent via e-mail along with two attachments.

I opened the first one and got a virus. After letting them know, I have never chosen to reconnect with this firm again. This experience left a terrible memory and a terrible negative impression, one which I did not care to revisit. I am glad this happened to me, so that I can be aware of and more closely monitor my own correspondence with respect to my own e-mail attachments.

To avoid these challenges, ask and alert the intended recipient before you send an attachment. In today's climate of heightened IT security, an unexpected attachment may be deleted and go unread. Also, it is good e-mail etiquette to ask in what format an attachment should be sent, to be sure this is easily downloaded as well as readable by the recipient. Avoid sending attachments that have complex artwork or high-resolution photographs imbedded within, because these take a long time to download and are often the cause of computer crashes. The last thing you want is to be remembered as the individual who sent a computer-crashing e-mail.

Overuse of graphics: Constantly improving technology means there are many news ways to add visual punch to your e-mail. There are dozens of "emoticons," variations of the smiley face, which can easily be inserted into e-mail text. There are programs that will embed your firm's logo into your e-mail or even a scanned version of your signature. My advice: Use these visuals sparingly. While some, such as the use of the corporate logo, are appropriate in business correspondence, others, such as a winking cartoon face, have no place in professional exchange. Still more lie in the gray area.

Use of a scanned signature, for example, is not, on the surface, wrong. However, it is not generally used in professional business correspondence.

E-MAIL TIPS

- Choose and use your subject line wisely. This is your opportunity to make a professional statement about yourself and a great first impression. Take care in word selection and be certain this opening line is spell checked and grammatically correct.

- Use honorifics. Even after invited to address someone by their first name, be careful using first names in e-mail correspondence. Be absolutely certain that anyone who happens upon this e-mail is okay knowing you call the company president by their first name.

- Include a personal greeting and a salutation to add warmth to impersonal e-mail communication.

- Respond promptly.

- Consider communications public domain, regardless of what is stated concerning confidentially. E-mail can be and is forwarded freely.

- Do not use e-mail correspondence in business communications to share jokes, chain mail, or other non-business-related banter.

- Do not send anything in an e-mail correspondence you would not post on a billboard in Times Square; there is no such thing as confidentiality.

- "Delete" never means gone forever. Be aware that even deleted e-mail is retrievable. Be sure all e-mail content is business appropriate.

- When using e-mail to schedule a meeting or resolve conflict, the rule is to revert to a more direct form of contact, such as the telephone or a personal visit after three exchanges on the same topic.

- Be sensitive to the fact that misunderstandings are common in e-mail communication. Be slow to take offense and quick to pick up the telephone. Know that e-mail may be misinterpreted or come across as crass, screaming, or lacking enough information.

- Do not use all capital letters UNLESS YOU WANT YOUR READER TO BELIEVE YOU ARE SCREAMING.
- Assume nothing. In this day of firewalls and spam filters, it is not unusual for an e-mail to be lost, undelivered, or inadvertently deleted. Do not assume lack of response is the response to your original message. Be prepared to follow up by another format such as telephone or fax if you are unsure.
- Never send an e-mail when angry. It is too easy to send a knee-jerk retort that is capable of having lasting ramifications and unwelcome repercussions. Although it is important to be prompt in responding, if an e-mail raises your blood pressure, wait 24 hours before replying and hitting "send." You may find the passage of the day cools your temper and allows for a more tempered response.

HOW TO RECOVER IF...

...you accidentally send an e-mail or document before it is ready for public viewing.

Work quickly. The sooner you get a revised version into the hands of your recipient, the better. Send the revised version as soon as possible and include in the subject line: "Kindly disregard previously sent document."

7

Dining Skills

Question: You invite a potential new customer out for lunch. Who decides where to dine? You or your prospect?

Answer: You decide. You have extended the invitation; therefore, you have both the responsibility and obligation to control this process. Consult the mutually respected third party for advice regarding the prospective client's favorite bistro or cuisine. It will certainly impress your prospect if you are able to make arrangements at her favorite restaurant. The willingness to research in advance and show attention to detail will speak in your favor.

There is nothing more ordinary than the business meal; however, whether much business is conducted or not, the table can be both an opportunity and a minefield. Here is a story to illustrate my point. A client hosted a staff dinner at an upscale restaurant in Boston. One young star with tremendous potential, a person being groomed to go on the road to represent the firm, made the fatal mistake of picking up his lobster bisque and drinking from the bowl. That single cup of soup cost the rising star his opportunity. His advancement was delayed. It was decided he was not yet ready.

The dining table is a great stage from which to share your personal side and demonstrate the respect you hold for your client or prospect. It is a moment when you can display your proper attention to etiquette, protocol, manners, and a myriad of details that can set you apart and distinguish you from the competition. At the same time, the dining table is also a forum for protocol faux pas. More than one position or business deal has been lost to mistakes made during a business meal. In fact, as a former member of the New England Human Resource Association, I learned that the third interview is one typically conducted over the table specifically to examine the applicant's manners. Employers want to know that the person they hire will not embarrass them with clients.

The execution of successful business meal etiquette begins long before the first course is served. Your efforts begin the moment you choose the restaurant. Etiquette suggests that whoever extends the invitation should select the restaurant, based upon knowing their guest's preference and restaurant of choice. Therefore, if I invite a new colleague or potential client to lunch, it is up to me to choose the restaurant, maintaining control. Use information you have gleaned regarding guests' preferences.

How do you know the preferred restaurant, particularly if this is a first-time luncheon with a new client? The best way to do this is through a third party—a mutual business acquaintance or a professional colleague. However, this is not the only route. You may ask the person's assistant or get creative and try and come up with another way to learn this information. It is worthwhile to begin this relationship on a note that demonstrates your attention to detail. If you are unable or cannot be bothered to find out, you probably do not deserve this luncheon opportunity.

Pre-planning Arrangements

There are arrangements the savvy professional should make in advance of the meal that will enhance your stature and impress your guest. Of course, make reservations, which helps diminish chances you will both be standing, waiting for a table, which is not good. Arrive a few minutes early in order to be able to greet your guest so she will not have to wait for you. This will give you the opportunity to meet and introduce yourself to your wait staff and pre-select your private or secluded table. Also, provide your credit card in advance in order to prearrange the check situation. By arriving early, you can preplan all arrangements to help ensure nothing less than a completely positive and successful dining experience.

Handling the Check Skillfully

Arrange in advance to pay the check when scheduling your reservation. This eliminates the awkward moment when the check arrives at the table, even though as host, it is assumed you are responsible. By calling or arriving in advance to give your credit card to the maitre d' or wait staff, you can arrange to have the bill taken care of without ever appearing at the table, thereby eliminating the awkwardness. Give the manager your credit card and say, "Under no circumstances should the bill be presented to the table." Instruct them to add 20% for the gratuity (more for better, less, accordingly). Excuse yourself at the end of dessert; no need to say where you are going. A simple "Excuse me" will suffice. Revisit the maître d', review and sign the check. This eliminates ever seeing a bill and thereby any awkwardness that might arise should the check be presented at the table.

This is a gracious and professional arrangement for which you can prepare in advance that will set you apart and highlight your ability to think ahead. Your preplanning activities in this regard will not go unnoticed. Plus, if you have ever done this, you may have also noticed that the proprietor, general manager, or maitre d' will stop by, perhaps multiple times, to check in on you. By arranging payment with such care and foresight, you have signaled to the restaurant staff that you are entertaining someone very special, someone of great importance. The staff, particularly in the hospitality industry, pick up on such nuances and act accordingly. This makes your guest feel very special and is a tremendously positive reflection on you. It is yet another step toward earning trust and respect and growing the relationship, which is your goal.

Seating Rules

Rule: Never be seated before your guest arrives. Wait in the reception area. Stand. Once your guest has arrived, let power-dining protocol begin. Regardless of gender, help guests with their coats. Regardless of gender, open the door and let them go first. Regardless of gender, permit guests to follow the maître d' first. (Important note for international travelers: In Europe, the host will always follow the maître d' first and take the seat at the far end of the room, facing the door. This is a European tradition, wherein the host walks through the dining area to scan the room for safety.) In the United States, hosts typically defer to guests of honor and allow them to proceed first. That said, most male clients I have encountered tend to be more traditional, and it has been my experience that gentlemen will invariably defer to me, allowing the women, then, to follow the maître d' first. How can you manage this moment with grace and aplomb? The woman host should offer or gesture once to her gentleman guest to proceed. After one gesture, woman hosts should graciously accept, rather than engage in the awkward dance of "No really, please, after you," "No, Judy, I insist, after you," or "No, I insist." The rule is this: After the initial gesture, it is appropriate for hosts, male or female, to accept the lead position and follow the maître d' first.

Once you have arrived at the table, give your guest the seat at the table with the best view or the most comfortable seat. Should you have a choice between sitting across the table from your guest or angular to them, you are encouraged to sit angular to your guest. Remember, you are endeavoring to grow the relationship. Sitting in an angular position eliminates the barrier of the table and helps encourage and cultivate personal rapport.

Once seated, do a time check. Ask your guest, "How are we for time today?" This allows your guest to let you know just how much time they have. Pace your time together, and alert wait staff accordingly, which is noticed and appreciated. You will be remembered well when you ensure your guest is on schedule for subsequent obligations. Once again, this is a positive reflection on you.

Please note: If you are moving from the networking area to the dining room, remeber to leave glasses—beer, wine, cocktails—behind. The reason? Presumably, your host has put in considerable time and effort in preselections and wine pairing.

Ordering

Suggest to your guest that you "get ordering out of the way" in order to be able to focus on relevant topics and each other. If not, you risk losing precious time you finally have together. How many times have you begun to chat, conversations ensue, the wait staff approaches to ask for your order and you say, "We have not even looked as yet." You resume banter, wait staff reappears, you are still not ready. Now, you are 15 to 20 minutes into your luncheon and you have not even ordered! By this time, perhaps up to one-third of your already limited time together has been eliminated. This is not good. Take control by suggesting early on that you order up front. This is efficient, and making this recommendation keeps you in control of the breakfast, lunch, or business dinner meeting.

The process of ordering is yet another great opportunity where you can shine, utilizing perfectly executed etiquette skill. Rule: Do not order the most expensive nor the least expensive items on the menu. Hosts have another opportunity here to shine. While reviewing the menus, set the tone and make your guest feel at ease. Rather than saying something tacky such as, "Feel free to order the most expensive thing on the menu. It's on the company," we suggest you consider saying something a bit more subtle, such as recommending various yet specific items on the menu in various price points. You might say, "I understand the salmon is outstanding here" or "I have tried the Porterhouse and it is terrific." Be sure to mention specific entrees in a full price range from the light salad or soup to pasta dishes to the filet mignon. This signals to your guest that they may indeed feel free to order anything they would like without considering cost.

For guests, the rule still applies: Order in the middle price range. Even when your host tells you to feel free to order whatever you might like, it is suggested that you not order the least nor the most expensive items on the menu. Show moderation and order anything in the middle price range.

The Order of Ordering

Ordering protocol suggests that the person of honor, seated to the hosts's right, order first, then ladies at the table order, then gentlemen, and finally, you, the host, should order last. Review this ordering protocol with your wait staff in advance to ensure they do not simply begin and move around the table in seating order. While this system may be easier and more efficient for them, as host, this is not your concern. Your concern is ensuring that the appropriate ordering process be upheld.

After you have all heard specials of the day, what may or may not be available on the menu, and ordering has begun, be sure to use proper phrasing. Please remember the three authoritative words when ordering: "I would like." Use them. Say, "I would like the escargot, and then I would like the rack of lamb." Use this rather than the often heard "Can I get..."

or "Can I have…" Of course you can! You are the customer! These weak phrases undermine your professionalism and suggest a more subservient role. Order authoritatively and decisively. This has a direct business tie in: You demonstrate authority and decisiveness at the table, so where else do you apply this skill? Bottom line: I want to do business with you. No one wants to do business with the person who seems unsure or subservient.

Question: Your guest has ordered the appetizer, soup, salad, and hot entree. You would like only a light salad. What should you do?

Answer: Match ordering, course for course, to help place your guest at ease. In this situation, it is appropriate to break the cardinal rule of childhood table manners and "play with your food." Eat what you can and subtly move food around a bit while your guest eats. Ordering should match course for course so the guest does not feel in any way awkward being watched or eating alone.

Question: Your guest would like to order a glass of wine. However, you do not care for one or you do not drink. What should you do?

Answer: When it comes to alcoholic beverages, there is no need to match your guest's ordering. Many people these days do not drink for many different reasons. That said, we suggest you consider ordering something more than simply tap water. Consider sparkling water, cranberry juice, an Arnold Palmer (half ice tea and half lemonade); anything with a lime is also good.

Ordering Wine

As host, it is your responsibility to order wine for the table. That said, if you know that one of your guests is a wine connoisseur and might appreciate the opportunity to shine a bit, it would be gracious to offer that person the spotlight.

Question: You have deferred the honor of ordering wine for the table to your guest. How do you keep a subtle yet firm hand on the cost and preventing him from ordering a terribly expensive bottle?

Answer: The host may quietly confer with the honoree and subtly refer to price points on the wine list, perhaps while making some suggestions, so that the other person understands the parameters. Or a little humor is always helpful: "My! We should all buy stock in that vineyard!" Either way, your challenge and responsibility as host is to control this process so that your guest does not get carried away and take advantage.

When to Give the 10-Minute Product Presentation

Often a business meal will have a brief pitch or product presentation. There are no hard and fast rules or right or wrong answers as to how and when this is addressed. However, if you wait until after lunch, you risk losing those who must leave. Mid-course may jeopardize interfering with the flow of your luncheon and conversation. Hence, we recommend that, about the time you order, suggest you spend the next 10 minutes or so providing a program overview so that should there be any questions, one can freely ask during the course of your luncheon. This also helps you control the course of the luncheon and your time together in order to help ensure you are making the most productive use of your time together, which is your raison d'etre. Be sure luncheon presentations are brief and concise.

Seating, Eating, Toasting

Guests: Be sure to watch your host and follow that person's lead. Nothing happens until or unless the host initiates it. This includes being seated (enter and exit from the chair's right; gentlemen assist ladies on their right with seating); saying grace (one should always be asked in advance); toasting; and beginning each course. Follow that person's lead. Once the host picks up her utensils, this is the signal that you may begin. Following your host's lead through the course of the dinner will keep you in correct protocol form.

Hosts must also be aware that their actions lead the rest of the table. Here is a story of what happens when the host forgets his leadership role. A president of one of my banking clients was hosting guests at his own table. Apparently, he became so engrossed in conversation with his person of honor that he and his conversation partner never ate. As a result, no one at their table ate. The president was never aware of any other guests at his table, never offered a toast, never, not once, picked up his utensils to begin and, out of respect, therefore, no one else at his table did either.

What could have been done in that situation? I would recommend passing the president a note or whispering a message in his ear signaling that he should begin. While guests appropriately and respectfully deferred to their host's lead, someone should have somehow gotten word to the president to begin. Even smiling and saying something lightly as a joke would have no doubt accomplished the task. Perhaps because of his title, people were more timid than they may normally have been had this has been someone else. Either way, what others, especially his guests, remember about that luncheon was this faux pas. It is better to be alerted discreetly, whether via use of humor or not, so the situation can be corrected without incident.

Grace

It seems that post September 11, 2001, many individuals, even during a business gathering, are offering grace before the meal. Here are some rules regarding the saying of grace: No napkin is touched, no water is sipped, no toast is proposed until after grace has been said. Keep your focus again on your host for this, as well as throughout the course of the meal. One should always be asked in advance so they can prepare something appropriate to say. Finally, grace should be brief and tailored to the audience.

Question: When does small talk cease and business discussion begin? Who initiates this transition?

Answer: Whoever initiated the luncheon is responsible for this segue. Generally speaking, however, business itself should not be discussed during luncheon. After luncheon, over coffee or dessert, it is appropriate to discuss business. In fact, most private clubs and many restaurants do not permit the use of laptops, cell phones, and other business tools while dining at the table. If you are seen raising your portfolio to take notes, you may be asked to put it away, as has happened for me.

Toasting

The topic of toasts is one that calls on several points of protocol. There are two types of toasts: one is less formal and is offered by the host at the start of the meal. The host may sit or stand, raise a glass, holding stem glasses by the stem with the first three fingers, not a fist. The host should look at each guest, make good eye contact, lean in toward the guests, and welcome and thank them for being present.

The second toast is more formal and is offered at the beginning of dessert. The host will rise and stand behind his chair. A glass, typically champagne, although wine or even water will do, is raised. Hold the champagne flute with the first three fingers at the top of the stem. A very elegant way to hold the flute is with the first three fingers at the base of the flute. Look at everyone at your table and engage them again with good eye contact and body language, and particularly focus on the person of honor, to whom you are toasting.

Number one rule regarding toasts: When the toast is being proposed in your honor, never drink to one's self.

After the host has offered the toast, he will be seated and everyone except the person of honor will drink. Etiquette suggests you need only touch glasses with those on either side of you. This said, if everyone at the table is doing a "skoll," crashing glasses together toward the center of the table with a big soccer cheer, by all means go along. I embrace the notion that the beauty in knowing the rules is knowing when it is okay to break them. Following the toast, the person of honor should rise, stand behind her chair, entering and exiting from the chair's right, also hold the glass appropriately, and graciously accept the beautiful toast, be seated, and, only then, drink.

Please note: We have all offered and accepted, and will continue to offer and accept, many toasts throughout the course of our professional careers, and personally as well. Please use toasting as an opportunity to shine. Please know this takes practice. Even if it is just speaking to and among your peers, many are unsure about what to say or simply do not feel comfortable speaking in front of others. It is wise to have something prepared in advance of any occasion where you believe there may be even the most remote chance you will be either proposing or accepting a toast.

An example of a simple, generic toast to which I remain partial: "I would like to propose a toast: to old friends and new! Cheers!" Or, this I heard from a good friend and business colleague: "Always reach toward the outer most edge of the branch, for this is where you will find the sweetest fruit." Take your time with the toast—this is your moment to shine. As always, warmth, sincerity, and eye contact go a long way in terms of being appreciated and well received.

The American vs. the Continental Styles of Dining

I am often asked, what is the difference? And, which is more acceptable? American and Europeans used to eat in exactly the same fashion in what is now called American style: fork in the left hand, knife in the right; cut and then rest the knife, serrated edge facing you on the plate, along the upper right of your plate, and then switch your fork from your left to your right hand. Swoop, rather than stab food into your fork and bring food into your mouth with your lips, not your teeth. Back and forth, continue cutting, resting the knife, switching the fork from the left to the right hand. (Left hand belongs in your lap while dining American style.)

The upper classes in Europe thought this was way too much work and in England, they simply stopped switching utensils. The Continental style of dining, suggests holding the fork and knife exactly the same way: fork in the left hand, knife in the right hand. Cut and then hold your knife in your right hand, resting your forearm (not your elbow) along the edge of the table. Leave the fork in your left hand, tines facing downward and then stab food with your fork. You can use your knife to help maneuver and secure small amounts of food onto the tines. Bring food into your mouth with your fork, in your left hand, tines facing downward, with your lips again, not your teeth.

There is no right or wrong or more correct form of eating. Neither is more correct. These are simply two styles of dining from two different regions of the world. Given the fact that we are global, it is wise to understand and know about both these styles of dining. Again, both are acceptable. Using both styles and switching during the course of the meal is quite appropriate.

An important dining note: It is inappropriate and quite rude to focus on cutting food and getting it into your mouth while your guest is talking or telling a story, particularly if the person is building up to a crescendo. Your sole focus should be on your guest and listening, not on your food.

Whichever style you follow, cut one or two small pieces at a time, leaving yourself free to open-ended questions. Please know that precutting an entire entrée is a practice reserved for children.

The Silent Service Code

To indicate that you have finished, there is the silent service code, which, if you look at the plate as a clock, one would position your utensils in the 10:20 position to signal "I am finished." This is the silent signal to the wait staff that indeed you have finished. Note: Tines are always down while eating European style and up if eating American style. Also, the cutting edge of the knife should face inward toward you, not out toward the glasses, and finally, fork is closest to you and the knife belongs on the right of the fork.

Special Situations

Not all business meals are created equal. Some are trickier to navigate then others. Here are a few specific situations you may encounter that require a particular level of attention to etiquette and protocol.

The Interview Lunch

Job applicants will often have their third and perhaps final interview in a restaurant. The reason for this: your prospective employer will know if you possess good table manners so you will not embarrass him when you dine with a client as a representative of his firm. Interview lunches are not like any other interview, nor are they like any other lunch you have ever had. They are auditions. It is not uncommon for the fate of the job applicant to rest on the performance or nonperformance at the interview table. So what do you need to know?

Question: Your food arrives and you know you enjoy tons of pepper on your salad or steak. Is it appropriate to pepper before tasting?

Answer: No. The rule is to never season your food until you taste it. Why? You are making the big decision before evaluating the details. "Does this require seasoning?" Human resource executives have shared with me they never hire anyone who seasons food before tasting. To them, this signals a level of hastiness and rush to judgment. Not all hiring managers are this focused on condiments; however, the story is instructive. It may look like a restaurant and you may believe this is a typical interview; however, it is really an extremely important audition. Your every move in each scene is under scrutiny.

This said, be prepared for hijinks at the interview lunch. Some employers use the interview lunch to test the job candidate's mettle. That may suggest the food and the service is rigged. Microsoft founder Bill Gates is known for doing this. In his writing, he has described his interviewing technique, which includes finding several equally qualified candidates, each with equally impressive credentials, and interviewing them over the dining table for a final decision. Bill Gates tells us that he will make challenges are presented in order to learn how the candidate conducts themself in situations, such as the applicant's steak arriving charbroiled and so rubbery that it is virtually inedible or something that is supposed to be sweet arriving sour or in some other way cooked incorrectly. Mr. Gates would then observe how the job candidate handles the situation. How does one, if at all, interrupt Bill Gates? Does one complain or remain stoic? Should the individual choose to be vocal, how does that person treat the wait staff? Does she show respect for the wait staff? Was the person authoritative or apologetic? Complicit? Rude? Arrogant? Indulgent? Direct? Gates believes this rite of passage offers him insights into how this person might behave under similar pressure on the job and interacting with people representing him. All these plants are ways in which Bill Gates is provided with further insight about this candidate that he might not otherwise have the opportunity to glean.

The Breadbasket

Here is the rule: Whoever is closest to the basket is responsible for helping themselves first, then offering to persons on the left, then, to the person on their right, then pass, left to right. Once you have your roll, resist the urge to break it in half, slather it with butter and nauche away. Rather, break off a small thumbnail-size bite over the bread and butter plate. Butter this piece over the plate, and pop this tiny piece into your mouth.

Why? Should you place a larger piece in your mouth and someone asks you an open-ended question, you might not be able to respond well. I have seen and personally experienced the awkward and embarrassing ritual of shaking one's head, chewing, swallowing, gulping, washing whatever-it-is down with water, and delaying the response. Remember once again, you are not there to eat. Be reminded to break the roll into a small, thumbnail-sized piece and eat one piece at a time.

Question: How should salt be passed?

Answer: Pass both the salt and the pepper, holding them with the first three fingers.

Jackets at the Table

The rule regarding jackets at the table is this: keep them on and buttoned. Appropriate dining protocol suggests that gentlemen and ladies should keep their jackets on and buttoned— the top two buttoned, the third open to vent—as one is seated at the dining and boardroom table. There are exceptions to this rule: if the room is warm, although if it is exceedingly warm and you may be embarrassed by removing your jacket, you may want to think twice. However, once again, hosts take the lead here. If your host removes his jacket, it would be acceptable for you to follow suit...so to speak.

Common Challenges and How to Effectively Deal With Them

Your food is terrible or not cooked to your satisfaction. How to deal with it? Sending it back is an option; however, it is not one generally recommended in business. I once attended a business dinner where one of the participants sent his steak back because it was undercooked. By the time the steak was cooked and represented at the table, the rest of the guests were beginning the dessert course. This steak may have been ultimately cooked properly; however, this was less than a positive reflection on this individual. Because he was not in sync with the rest of the table, the absence of the entrée was conspicuous and distracting.

Once again, none of us are gathered at the business dining table to eat. Therefore, should an instance such as this occur, I encourage you to keep your entrée and eat around it: eat the vegetables and mashed potatoes, use lots of resting positions, moving your food around, sip your beverage, and focus your attention on business conversation; you can eat later.

Excusing One's Self From the Table

One need only say "Excuse me" to persons with whom they are speaking. There is no need to say where you are going or why. When a lady excuses herself from the dining table gentlemen should rise out of respect.

Situation: A woman rises to excuse herself and no one, including the host, rises. Should you rise, risking showing up the host? If you do not, you risk insulting the woman and lowering your own high standards of conduct and behavior.

Solution: Use the half-seat: Rise halfway from your chair in order to show respect to the woman as she excuses herself and returns to the table, and to maintain your own high standards without showing up your host or anyone else at the table. This gesture will be greatly appreciated and noticed in a positive way.

Handling the Check

The arrival of the check can often be an awkward moment. The best way to handle this: Arrange in advance with the manager to have the amount plus a gratuity billed to your credit card. Be sure the check never arrives at the table. This is a skillful and polished way to manage a potential hiccup.

You come to gristle in your meat. What to do? The rule is this: The way it goes in is the way it comes out. Therefore, if you used your fork to take this unfortunate bite, discreetly plate this gristle on your fork and then onto your plate. Resist the urge to call attention to what you are doing. There is no need to say, "Excuse me, everyone, this is going to be disgusting. Please, don't watch." Simply place the gristle onto your fork and onto the side of your plate, without comment or incident.

Suppose you drop your utensil. If you are in a restaurant, ask your waiter to replace it. If you are in someone's home, pick up the utensil yourself. This should still be replaced.

Suppose you have lost your waiter. Often, waiters disappear at the most inopportune moments, however there is a right and a wrong way to get their attention. The right way: Simply raise one hand, holding the index and third finger aloft. It is not appropriate to snap one's fingers or shout out "Hey!" or even "Garcon!" Treating wait staff with respect is tantamount. Do endeavor to know your wait staff's name and use it. Also, do not go in search of your waiter. If you are truly in a bind, get the attention of another member of the restaurant staff and ask that wait staff to have your wait staff come to your table.

Suppose your wait staff begins to clear your table before everyone at the table is finished. Actually, this incident should never occur. Particularly if this is an important dinner, you might want to review this with your wait staff in advance, to ensure it does not occur. However, should this happen, and it does, as always, it is not what you say, however how it is said. You do not want to embarrass your server, who is trying to be efficient, perhaps does not know, or may have forgotten. Use the name of your waiter and say, "Why don't we wait until everyone has finished eating before we clear the table?"

BUSINESS DINING TIPS

First, please know that ordering anything challenging, such as ribs, finger food, lobster, and even pizza, can be a potential hazard. Remember, you are not there to eat. Consider ordering easy-to-eat items during this business meal.

- A hamburger: Eat it like sandwich. Cut it in half or even quarters.

- Pizza: Using a fork and knife is never wrong and is easier to manage, particularly if pizza has multiple toppings. Authentic Italian style suggests folding the triangular piece, like a sandwich, and eating from the smallest point to the crust.

- Soup: Hold the spoon like a pencil. Spoon away from your body and lightly tap excess soup from the spoon onto the outer edge of your soup bowl. Sip the soup from the side, not the point of the spoon; no slurping or blowing to cool down, and no dunking bread, either.

- Fish knife: Hold this like a pencil and fold the delicate fish onto the tines of the fork; no need to "saw" delicate fish.

- Napkins placed as a bib around your throat: This applies to small children; adults should refrain from such a practice.

- Lobsters: Bib or no bib? For lobsters, a bib is acceptable. In fact, many restaurants will go to great lengths to ritually place the bib on their guest and make every effort to help prevent potential disasters that typically occur when eating lobster, unless you are very adept.

- Donuts: Dunking donuts in coffee is reserved only for the privacy of your own home.

- Sauces: It is permissible to soak up sauces with your bread and enjoy, however, as always, there is a way to do so. Once again, break off a thumbnail-size piece from your bread. Pierce this with your fork and then swab the special sauce.

- Condiments: Ideally they should be served in a container with a small spoon. Use the spoon to place condiments on your plate. Dip into the condiments on your plate, not the service container.

- Salad: Ideally, salad should be prepared so that lettuce need not be cut; however, if not, it is acceptable to use your salad knife.

- Bread and butter: Break roll into thumbnail-size pieces, one at a time. Butter one piece at a time over the bread and butter plate with your personal butter spreader. Unwrap butter over the bread and butter plate. Use your butter spreader to scrape butter off the foil. Fold the foil in half and place under your bread and butter plate.

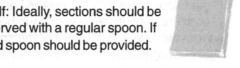

- Grapefruit half: Ideally, sections should be precut and served with a regular spoon. If not, a serrated spoon should be provided.

HOW TO RECOVER IF...

...the food or service is poor.

This should never occur because you will have done due diligence in preselecting the restaurant in advance, based on your client's preference. However, should this occur, proceed with the lunch. Avoid confrontations or complaints to managers in front of clients. Accept responsibility and apologize on behalf of the establishment. Use this as an opportunity to schedule another luncheon meeting to make this up to your client.

8

Presentations

Presentations are an integral part of business life. While some are informative and captivating, many are tortuous. We have all endured many more presentations than perhaps we would like. We have learned much from the great presentations. We learn still more from those that fall flat. As we all endeavor to give memorable, professional presentations, our goal must be to both create a positive learning experience for our audience and get our message across effectively. Etiquette and protocol play a vital role toward this effort because they set you apart. Executing stellar presentations invites yet another opportunity for you to distinguish yourself. Mastering the art of presenting takes awareness and much practice. Remember always, it is the nuances, the little things one employs during both preparation and execution, which will most positively impact your audience.

Executing a stellar presentation begins long before you say hello at the podium. Prepare and know your material; own it. Rehearse so you no longer need cue cards. This can make or break your ultimate effectiveness. Here is a story in which preparation and owning one's material overcame all other factors in the presentation. I was asked to critique a mayoral debate of two candidates. The incumbent was a seasoned, polished professional. He dressed impeccably for the debate and looked fabulous. However, when it came time for the three-minute recap at the close of the debate, he read every word from his notes.

By contrast, his opponent was a bit of a renegade. This debate was most likely the first occasion in a long while for which this gentleman, his opponent, had sported a tie. And even though the opponent wore an ill-fitting suit, a loud tie, and tan construction boots at the debate, his demeanor through the debate and his critical closing remarks were spoken confidently, with heart, without referencing one note or cue card. His delivery was heartfelt and he thoroughly won over the audience. Even though he did not look the part, he clearly stood apart. Why? He owned his material and when he spoke, everyone listening felt his sincerity. He knew his information. He was precise, accurate with every fact, figure, date, and his opponent's record. He engendered credibility, trust, confidence, and won my vote as victor of that debate. It is critical toward earning trust that you own your material. As one of my esteemed clients and good friend once reminded me, "The moment your audience senses weakness, you are dead." Not owning your material in order to present confidently will cost you your credibility.

Another aspect of preparation: Particularly if you are presenting to a intimate crowd, perhaps at a seminar or anything smaller than an auditorium, try to obtain a list of the attendees in advance. This will allow you to prepare both in content, by knowing the background and potential interests of your audience, and in delivery. By reading the list in advance, you have the opportunity to practice saying the names of your audience members. This will surely help you stand apart as a presenter. Your audience will know that you are not just presenting your routine material; rather, you have custom tailored this to them.

Technology

Prepare your technology. Check the mechanics of all visual aids, including Power Point, flip charts, sound system, and audio/visual equipment. Mechanical malfunctioning during your presentation is a poor reflection on you. I once attended a presentation where technical malfunctioning contributed to 30 minutes of down time, which ultimately failed the presenter.

Attire

Your appearance is critical in how you are perceived and received by your audience. Like it or not, you will be judged on how you look. Therefore, look the part. This is an important first step. I make it a rule to dress professionally, which, in some cases, may mean dressing up a notch from my audience. Given that you are the expert, your audience looks up to you. High standards of excellence in every aspect of your visual presentation are important. While business casual is acceptable in some companies these days, I believe a presenter, coming into a company as an outsider, out of respect, one has the responsibility to look professional. Your attire should convey your professionalism as the authority in your field.

Another reason to pay careful attention to your attire: Once you have done so, you are less likely to be worried or even think about how you look when you present. Once fully confident that you are appropriately dressed, you will not be distracted and can conduct your presentation and impart your message with confidence and authority. Chapter 11 is devoted to attire; however, here are some basics of dressing for a presentation.

Choose quality and dark, professional colors: For men and women, colors such as navy blue, dark grey, pinstripe, and black are appropriate. While a three-piece suit is not necessary, and in fact, these days, considered somewhat over the top, a suit and tie is never wrong. Women should choose a suit or pantsuit, not a jacket and slacks. Skirts are still considered the most professional.

Wear business professional shoes: Remember that if you are on a stage, your audience will have a direct view of your feet. For men: the black, presidential tie. For women: classic pumps; no open toes or sling backs.

After making your conservative attire choices, you may find when you arrive at your presentation site that the dress code is more relaxed than you anticipated. It is always easier to dress down. Certainly, much easier and less stressful than arriving and finding you are underdressed for your event.

Here is a story that illustrates my point. I remember being in Florida at an upscale hotel conducting training. Virtually every woman on staff was wearing sling back heels, considered one of the top two taboos with respect to shoes for women in business. When I inquired about this to my direct contact, she told me that sling back shoes there were considered completely acceptable. After having been completely reassured, I then gratefully changed my shoes to wear my sling back shoes with confidence. Remember, the beauty in knowing the rules is knowing when it is okay to break them. I asked and decided to break the rules in order to connect/mirror and adapt to my audience. The rest of my attire was still completely business professional.

Business Casual

While at one time it may have been appropriate to dress in more casual attire in order to fit in with a company whose culture was blue jeans and a tee shirt, today, post dot.com bubble, many firms have returned to and embraced business professional for two reasons: Business casual attire has been thoroughly abused in business, and it has been found that one's lackadaisical attire is reflected in their lackadaisical work performance. Interestingly, I was privy to an article distributed by the Associated Press wherein 100 random companies that spanned disciplines throughout the country participated in an experiment. They agreed to change their firm's formal business dress code to business casual for one year. The firms included CPAs, attorneys, manufacturing firms, engineers, financial services companies, and so on. At the end of one year, across the board, 99 out of 100 firms agreed to return to business professional for two reasons: (1) Business casual had been abused; tank tops, bare midriffs, and so on were rampant. (2) Perhaps more importantly, they confirmed that one's lackadaisical attire was reflected in a lackadaisical work performance.

It is unlikely you will be considered overdressed if you wear professional business attire. Of course, dress according to your topic of expertise. For example, if you are an expert in crickets and crocodiles and you are making a presentation on that topic, khakis as the uniform of choice would be appropriate. However, if your business is finance, taxes, or marketing, your attire should reflect the mode of your expertise and the professional standards you and your firm represent.

Other Important Preparation Tips:

☞ Visit the rest room and be confident you are in perfect order.

☞ Arrive early so you can check everything in the room.

☞ Stand at the door and personally greet and shake hands with each attendee as he or she arrive. Shaking hands provides you with valuable information in sizing up your audience, which will help empower you during your presentation. You will get a pulse on who is nervous and who prefers to be kept at a distance. Who is eager and energized, looking forward to the presentation? Who wishes they were anywhere else? These individuals are your most immediate challenges. Embrace them!

Each audience is different; therefore, each presentation is different, and you need to completely customize and adapt your presentation to each audience. Feel comfortable with room setup and mechanics, own your material, look fabulous and professional, and begin the act of presenting. Your challenge with each presentation: to win over your audience.

Project energy and enthusiasm! You are excited, delighted to be there! This is contagious! We as human beings are naturally drawn toward positive energy. Being genuinely thrilled to be there and grateful for the opportunity to share information that you believe will help your audience is key. Be sincere. Sincerity comes across through your behavioral style, body language, and eye contact or lack thereof. People can sense if this is forced or contrived in any way. If an audience senses weakness, they will prey on it! You are dead. I know. This has happened to me.

Visual = 55%

Verbal = 38%

Content = 7%

55%   38%

7%

Therefore, energy and enthusiasm from out of the gate are critical in order to engage and retain your audience. Remember, 38% is how you say it.

When the presentation begins:

☞ Stand and listen to your introduction.

☞ Shake hands with the introducer. Often, an introduction is a litany of your accomplishments. Accept this moment of praise and attention graciously.

☞ Stand. Pause and allow your audience to view you from head to toe. Wait five to 15 seconds. Women should wait even a little longer.

☞ Thank those who introduced you and invited you. Make eye contact with each as you say his or her name. Thank everyone in attendance for taking the time to attend and investing time with you.

☞ Remove your watch. This is to avoid the small but deadly sin of noticeably checking the time during your presentation. There is nothing more off-putting than seeing the presenter glance at his watch. Why? However unintentional, even though you may simply be trying to keep your time line, this suggests that you might be anxious to leave or somehow do not truly want to be there. You may recall the famous George Bush / Bill Clinton presidential debate wherein President Bush looked at his watch. The image beamed and perception was implanted forever through the airwaves of our country. This simple gesture severely compromised President Bush's credibility. No one remembers one thing about that debate with respect to substance or content. All they remember was President Bush checking the time on his watch. This was a small but extremely costly faux pas from which we can all take a cue.

Still, it is critical to keep track of time during your presentation. If you are fortunate, there is a clock in the room or a thermometer graphic that indicates how much time or how many slides remain. Know where this is or refer to your watch, off your wrist and accessible on a front table, so you can keep track of time and keep on schedule. Use whatever means you have to help you keep track of the time; this is critical. There is nothing worse than running over time and taking others valued time.

Once underway:

☞ Opening remarks: Humor still works as a wonderful way to help place your audience at ease and, build an immediate connection. This said, a joke or humorous story that has no connection to topic will not help you. Be careful with delivery. Not everyone can deliver naturally or well. Know if you fall into this category and may need extra practice in this important area. There is nothing worse than being flat or foul, particularly at kickoff. Try your opening remarks out on a test audience before using them in a presentation and see how they play.

☞ Introduce your material. Provide an overview of what your audience can expect; remember, you are endeavoring to build trust, earn the right to advance, and develop a relationship. Make them aware of what to expect. Ask permission to advance.

☞ Get off the stage. Whenever possible, I try to dismount and get off the stage early—right away, thereby eliminating the stage as a barrier. This enables me to better connect with my audience.

☞ Use a lavaliere microphone or an earpiece versus a handheld microphone. When you can walk in and among your audience and use your hands, you are more effective, can make better direct contact, stimulate more energy, and generate stronger audience participation. It is easy for an audience to tune out a talking head on a remote stage and much more difficult to ignore the person walking right by your chair, asking a direction question using that person's name, read from their name badge you can see.

Visual Aids and PowerPoint for
Any Presentation

Where should you stand? When you think about it, which way do people read? From left to right, yes? Therefore, we suggest you consider standing to the left of your visual aids, as your audience views you, in order to help ensure that their first visual is *you*. Any visual aid such as PowerPoint, overheads, handouts, and so on, should be regarded as little more than props. These should not be the focal point of your presentation; you are.

Oftentimes, presenters believe that use of multiple visual aids or props will enhance their overall effectiveness, when in fact for many they detract from optimum impact. Remember, your challenge is to engage your audience as an energetic, vibrant, enthusiastic, sincere presenter with a formidable personal style. This, rather than project an image of a slide from your projector.

Note regarding PowerPoint: Never read your slides as part of your presentation. There is little more insulting than to ask others to invest their time attending your presentation, only to have that presenter literally read each slide, word for word. Your audience can read!

Your most important asset: your eyes. Use your eyes to directly connect with the eyes in your audience. Start from the person at the farthest part of the room, plant your eyes and connect with theirs; complete the thought. Move your gaze to another at the far end of the room, plant your eyes; complete the thought. Your challenge is to make each person feel as though as you are speaking directly to him or her.

When done well, this is a remarkable technique. I was in a ballroom of 800 people when President Clinton gave the keynote at the National Academy Foundation in Anaheim. President Clinton, who as former Governor of Arkansas used to literally fumble walking up to the podium, stumble over his words, and was mocked and ridiculed mercilessly by the press. Today, President Clinton is by far and away the most engaging (and highest paid) public speaker in the country because he has cultivated and developed the technique of making every person in any room feel as though he is talking to and connecting directly with him. This has become his signature, his personal style, even in a room with 800 people.

Do not chance-gaze; rather, meet the gaze of one individual, complete your thought, and then move on to another individual and complete the thought. Endeavor to make eye contact with everyone in the room. Follow the one-thought/one-person strategy. This will help each person with whom you connect feel you are talking directly to them. The most effective presenter will endeavor to draw the audience in toward them. Begin by making eye contact with the person farthest away, then work you way in toward you.

Your eyes are important messengers to your audience, even when you are not looking at them. Be aware that your eyes can travel when you are speaking and when you listen and respond to questions and comments. Eyes looking up at the sky or ceiling suggests "Heaven help me," not an authoritative image. Looking sideways may suggest you are a bit shifty or untrustworthy. Looking down and pausing shows you are a thoughtful person, intent upon imparting the correct response. Looking down is more suggestive of a pensive person.

Practice using your eyes, just as you would practice giving your speech. I remember when I first began my seminars, I would practice the art of making eye contact. I would line up my three dogs, my 2-year-old son in his high chair, and various photographs of friends and family that I would place randomly throughout the room. I would try to make direct eye contact with each one. It worked! Yes, I felt even my dogs were reading me! Practice, even though these sessions were not with a real audience, and this exercise truly helped me.

Try to keep your hands quiet. Gesturing should be kept at a minimum. While you do not want to keep arms robotically at your side, overdoing grandiose hand movements can be distracting. Although excessive use of hands and gesturing is acceptable in certain countries, generally speaking, overdoing hand movements can be distracting. Keep this to a minimum.

Maintain a correct professional standing position. Be aware of how your movements affect your presentation. Weave or wend your body into your audience rather than standing perfectly erect or leaning back and seeming distant or aloof, which is also suggestive of keeping others at a distance rather than drawing them in.

Answering Questions

"That's a good question" or "Now that's a terrific question" are commonly said retorts when presenters receive questions. However, I once had someone in my seminar share with me a nuance I would like to share here with you. He said someone in his audience responded, "I didn't know I was being graded." Therefore, when responding to any question, we suggest the presenter say, "Thank you for your question," and then proceed to authoritatively answer it. With a larger audience, you may need to repeat the question first and then proceed. The perception of rating or grading a question suggests that the other person's question wasn't great.

Be aware of your voice and all aspects of it—texture, volume, tonal quality, inflections, and so on. While the visual aspects of your presentation make the most impact, the second most important element is verbal, what the audience hears. Therefore, it is not as much what we say rather how we say it. Your voice is your primary tool in the audio portion of any presentation. How you use your voice is virtually as important as your visual.

Pay attention to articulation. Be careful not to swallow your words. Speak clearly, distinctly. Articulate. This takes practice. Practice not only in front of a mirror, but also practice reading your speech or presentation, even a poem, in one room. Ask a friend or colleague to listen from another room next door. This will force you to annunciate and articulate your words and practice listening yourself, to the sound of your own voice, something with which we are not always comfortable.

Sometimes, even extreme practice can pay off on presentation day. When my son was in the fourth grade, he had a public speaking assignment. Each member of his class was going to speak in the school auditorium in front of all the parents. To practice, his assignment was to recite, by memory, his speech and practice saying this from another room in order to articulate and accurately project words and his voice to be heard from the next room. Although while practicing, this may have seemed exaggerated and overdone, ultimately, this proved to be invaluable, as he and every member of his class delivered their speeches most admirably.

Work hard to help ensure a rich tonal quality. A cold or squeaky tone, a tired or dry voice is a turnoff. Be sure you and your voice are well rested and fresh. Project a strong, confident voice and your message with energy, warmth, and sincerity. This will resonate by virtue of the tone you are conveying. Use tonal quality as a means to create connection with your audience.

Consider an often overlooked tool: pausing. Because approximately 95% of all adults are nervous or anxious prior to any meeting or presentation, many tend to rush. Please be aware of the positive impact you will have in slowing down and pausing occasionally, because this will allow you to emphasize key points. The quiet moment may seem like an eternity to you; however, to your audience, this is simply a minor break in the action and a moment to ponder and reflect upon that which has been said.

Beware the nonwords. Eliminate the "um," "you know," "like," and "I mean." These are all filler phrases many of us use in casual conversation; however, they have no place in a professional presentation. They dilute your message, have a negative impact, and suggest that the presenter is either young, inexperienced, nervous, or simply not well prepared. Nonwords are typically nervous distractions. I heard a story where a presenter was well prepared and had terrific content, but so consistently used the expression "and whatnot" that audience members phased out content and started counting the "and whatnot"s. Clearly, this was not the intended goal of the presenter.

Other Word Choice Tips

1. Avoid using "you guys." Refer to the audience as "ladies and gentlemen."
2. Use "thank you" instead of "thanks."
3. Use "yes" rather than "yeah."
4. Use "however" rather than "but."
5. Say "I believe" rather than "I think."
6. Use "thank you for the question" rather than "that's a great question.

Do not get carried away by the technologies now available for presentations. Many are quite helpful. However, too many can be distracting to your audience. The bells and whistles can often overwhelm a presentation and camouflage the point. I attended a presentation where the speaker showed some great clips from various movies. The clips were fun and encouraged much conversation among us regarding the movie, how good or not we felt it was. However, in an attempt to get his point across by showing these clips, in reality, the same clip could have been shown for two to three minutes rather than his 10 to 15 minute time intervals. This is valuable time taken away from the audience and the presentation, which I resented. I felt that I did not invest this time and make this financial investment in attending this seminar to be entertained or to revisit old movies. I resented this poor attempt at trying to entertain during the seminar. They even served popcorn during this 9 a.m. sales presentation!

There is much to be said for the old-fashioned flip chart and easel, of which you have total control. However, a word of caution prior to using them: Know you audience. Should your audience have a preference for a technological overlay, by all means, step up. I was preparing to address an audience of college students and it was made clear that PowerPoint instead of a flip chart and easel would be required as a key component of my delivery. A big pad of paper and a colored marker would perhaps not necessarily be the most effective medium in which to most directly connect with this highly technologically oriented group of young adults. The flip chart and easel would seem less serious and ultimately have less impact to this generation raised in the high technology age. Of course, I took the cue and adapted my presentation to my audience accordingly. Every audience is different. Know your audience, know their culture and mentality, and adjust your medium accordingly.

When presenting, endeavor to put your audience at ease. Consider these tips:

☞ Announce the schedule and tell them what you are going to tell them.

☞ Make your audience aware of when breaks are scheduled.

☞ Announce if and when there will be time allotted for questions and answers.

Remember, here too you are endeavoring to earn respect and build trust, earning the right to advance and connect with your audience. Your goal is to adapt to each audience, engage with a theme, and capture their attention to share and impart knowledge. You as a presenter can learn much valuable information from every audience, by their reactions to you, the stories you share, and by their questions, as do I.

Engaging Your Audience

Is your audience engaged? Are they with you? Read and be aware of glazed eyes. Read their body language; are they slumping, nodding, or leaning forward in their seats? Are they checking e-mail and texting on their handheld devices? Know when to take an unscheduled break. Should you begin to feel you are in danger of losing your audience, do something unpredictable such as an exercise to get them re-engaged, or take an unscheduled break. Once again, know when to break the rules.

Question: What do you do if your audience is wandering or one person appears clearly bored or is just being obnoxious? This can to happen from time to time.

Answer: Embrace the opportunity. Confront the situation and this individual head on. Engage the person. Ask questions. Involve the person in a role-play. Make that person feel special. It works.

Concluding

Bringing your fabulous presentation to its conclusion takes forethought. Plan what you want to say and tie this in to something specific pertaining to this audience. You will need to consider this prior to the actual conclusion of your presentation. When concluding, of course, be gracious. Thank your audience for coming, for their valuable time and attention, and participation (if appropriate). Again, thank the individuals who invited you and those who introduced you. Mention the assistant and/or individuals who helped make this event possible. Be sure to look at each person as you say his name. Be genuine, sincere. When delivering your conclusion and thank yous, a slight bow is also appropriate.

Proceed to the door and shake hands with each individual. Thank them personally again for coming and for their time. Use their name as you say farewell, if you remember this, or reference their name badge. This gesture of personally walking attendees to the door, shaking their hand once again, and thanking them for attending is a mark of a true professional and demonstrates your genuine respect and appreciation. You have been endeavoring to earn trust, develop a rapport with your audience, and hopefully you have been successful. Not taking this extra step completely negates everything you have been working so hard to accomplish and sends mixed signals to your audience. While they may not expect you to go this extra step, this completes the essence of what you have been endeavoring to accomplish and have hopefully achieved.

Remaining at the conclusion of your presentation to interact with your audience leaves a positive impression. Certainly, sprinting for the door can give the opposite image. I attended a seminar where the presenter made his grand entrance after everyone had been networking in advance. No one had a chance to shake his hand or speak with him one on one other than during the course of his presentation. Interestingly, he exited just as quickly following his presentation! And his presentation was all about the art of sales and persuasion skills! I was not persuaded.

 WHAT TO DO IF...

...your technology fails you.

Be prepared to move on without it. Remember, technology is a prop, which is fine. However, if you are so dependent upon it that you cannot proceed without it, you have placed your presentation and your professional credibility in jeopardy.

...you sneeze, cough, and so on.

The rule regarding bodily functions is: Turn away from your audience. This holds true for any bodily function, including taking a drink of water. Remember that even if you have turned away, your microphone may still pick up the audio. Here is a story to illustrate my point. There was once a presenter who was miked, who excused herself from her seminar, went into the ladies room, and did not turn off her microphone. Needless to say, this was not well received.

My brother spoke to a group where I was in attendance and i watched and listened as he gulped down a glass of water at the podium—right in front of the microphone! He didn't turn away!

...your audience looks bored.

Take your own energy up a notch. Convey through voice and body language that you are high energy and this will be contagious. Change up subject matter and your physical positioning in the room. Your efforts to regain control and command attention will be realized. Or, you can try an unscheduled role-play to get the audience re-involved or call an unscheduled break to regroup

...turning away.

When writing on a board or easel or otherwise needing to turn away from your audience in any way, say "Please excuse my back."

...your audience is talking.

Stand authoritatively, and pause; make eye contact, project a clear, confident, authoritative "Excuse me for interrupting. Welcome back!" Lead by example, by demonstrating proper etiquette in your own demeanor and professional decorum.

...you run out of time.

Going over your allotted time a little is understandable. Going over the time set by a wide margin will work against you. You want to be remembered as the person with the wonderful presentation, not as the individual whose speech went so long everyone had to miss lunch. Be respectful of your audience's time.

PRESENTATION TIPS

- Be well rested.
- Be so well prepared that cards and notes are unnecessary; own your material.
- Dress appropriately.
- Arrive early.
- Shake hands with everyone if possible and personally welcome your audience.
- Shake hands with your introducer.
- Take off your watch.
- Make eye contact with the individual furthest from you first, and then work your way in one individual at a time.
- Be aware of voice quality, projection, pacing, and volume.
- When using PowerPoint or other props, stand to the left. Because your audience reads from left to right, the focus will be on you.
- Be mentally engaged and physically relaxed, and let your creative substance shine through.
- Conclude graciously, with a slight bow.
- Walk to the door and personally thank each person for coming.

9

The Meeting

You have finally scored the big meeting with a great, potential new client. You arrive in the conference room and take your place at the table. You wait for your host to be seated and then you take your seat.

Question: What do you do with your hands? On the table or in your lap? Does it matter?

Answer: Keep them on the table where they can be seen. The derivation of the term "underhanded" comes from ancient times when concealing one's hands might have meant you were concealing a weapon. While there's little chance that fellow meeting goers will worry that you are armed and dangerous, keeping your hands in view makes it clear that you are aboveboard and not hiding anything. This also looks much more professional.

When it comes to taking the meeting, take nothing for granted. This is your moment and you will need all your etiquette tools to shine, outdistance your competition, and create connection and trust. Meetings happen so often in business life that often we might instinctively tend to gloss over the finer tuning and simply barrel ahead with little regard to the nuances that proper protocol provides. Please consider this: You have most likely gone to considerable time and effort to secure the meeting in the first place. You have networked, researched, pitched, presented, and maneuvered to be here. It stands to reason that you would want to use every tool at your disposal to make this meeting successful and use this opportunity to distinguish yourself. There are many ways that the use of proper etiquette and protocol can make this happen.

Getting the Meeting

The first opportunity you have to demonstrate your superior etiquette skills is how you go about getting this important meeting. Many will tell you this requires subterfuge, bribing the assistant or somehow getting in tight with the gatekeeper to get on "*the* schedule." This may or may not result in a meeting; however, this will certainly not help you to build trust or confidence within this organization. Any time you resort to bribery, misrepresentation, or false pretenses, you jeopardize the trust factor and sever the connection you so endeavor to enable.

Others will say that getting the impossible meeting with the much-sought-after client requires larger-than-life theatrics. I heard the president and CEO of a major furniture retail store give a presentation on how she was able to break into the furniture business when she had never held a job in her life. She saw a position advertised in the newspaper for a floor manager in a furniture showroom and had it in her head that she would be fabulous at this, and she wanted the job. However, she was unable to get an interview and was having trouble getting the attention of the firm's president. She called, left messages and more messages. She faxed. She wrote letters. She begged his receptionist to help her get an interview. She knew if she could just get in front of this man, he would hire her. She would be able to convince him that she was the right person for this position. However, she could not get this first meeting. Finally, she had an incredibly original idea to get his attention.

She had no money and so took a line of credit from her credit card and hired a plane to fly over the company head-quarters with a banner that read: "Please meet with Jane Doe." She called his secretary and asked her to have him look out his window at 12:05 p.m. He did. When he saw this, he appar-ently shook his head and acquiesced. She got the meeting and the job.

This is a great story; however, this level of theatrical effort (and cost!) is not necessary to obtain most meetings today. The best way to secure the difficult-to-get meeting with the much-sought-after individual is through a mutually re-spected third party. This is why investing time in networking is so critically important. This is also why you should never write anyone off as not worth your time at a networking event. You never know. You may feel that individual is not valuable to you right at that moment in time. However, a time may come when you discover that individual is the childhood friend, golf partner, or trusted vendor of the very person you would like to meet. Networking is the crucial stepping-stone to se-curing any difficult-to-get meeting.

When does the meeting really begin? Much sooner than most people realize. The meeting begins the moment you first have the individual on the telephone. Even though you are not yet face to face, consider this your first meeting. You are, in fact, meeting at this very moment through your voice. When making arrangements for the meeting via telephone, be sure you project energy, confidence, professionalism and warmth in your voice. Do not save your personal or professional best for the face-to-face meeting; start now. Consider using all the skills shared in Chapter 5: smile (use a mirror to help you achieve a pleasant expression, and permeate the wires); stand when speaking to ensure strong projection of voice and purpose. Do these things even if you are simply leaving a voice-mail message. This is your first opportunity to "brand" yourself and your firm, and to be remembered positively or not. This first moment communicating with your much-sought-after potential client is critical; make it count.

The day of the meeting, remember, the meeting itself begins the moment you arrive on company site. As soon as you drive into the parking lot, they own you. Particularly with heightened security these days, you never know where cameras are and who may be watching. As soon as you drive onto company property, you need to be in meeting mode, fully focused. Far too often, business professional fail to treat the arrival on property as meeting time. Incidentally, every faux pas of which I speak herein, I have committed. This is one of them.

Here's the story: I arrived at my client's office building, on property, drove up to the building and parked my car. I then proceeded to prepare: I changed shoes, fixed my hair, checked my makeup, used some mint breath spray, made a few quick phone calls, all in the car before I went in to meet with my client. After I entered the building and walked into his office I sat down and looked out his office window; there was my car! He had seen everything I was doing! I was so embarrassed!

I had another experience much later on in my career, when I arrived at my meeting site and the building was massive. So, never dreaming that I would be viewed, I was again arranging my papers, taking care of last-minute things in my car, and collecting myself. I started to look for the building number of my meeting site when my cell phone rang. "Hello Judy, you need to walk down two more entrances to get to my section of the building." My client could see me thanks to security cameras that beamed images to an intranet Website. You must be in full meeting mode from the moment you enter the property. You are not backstage; you are on stage.

Once you are out of the parking lot and in the lobby, the next phase of meeting etiquette rules are in effect. When you announce yourself to the receptionist present your business card, writing side up so that it does not require being turned around to be read. This is a professional courtesy to the receptionist or gatekeeper because this helps facilitate her job to properly and efficiently announce and connect you to your party. By presenting your card when you greet him, using his name (on the desk or a badge), you avoid having the person mispronounce your name, or asking again, "Who did you say you were with?" "How do you spell that?" Your card helps the gatekeeper be more efficient in announcing you.

Once you have been announced, ask the receptionist for directions to the nearest rest room. Do a final once-over on your appearance: hair, makeup, clothes, breath, and so on. Be sure to wash and dry your hands so that handshakes will be free of clamminess.

When you return to the reception area, you are informed that the individual with whom you are meeting has been detained 15 or 20 minutes. You are invited to take a seat in their luxurious, beautifully appointed reception area and make yourself comfortable.

Question: Should you take advantage of this gracious gesture?

Answer: I recommend against taking advantage of the gesture extended by this clearly well-trained, very efficient receptionist. Even though you are told it might be 15 to 20 minutes, how many times have "they" come down in more like five? Then you have been caught relaxing or multitasking, either way suggesting that what you are doing takes precedence over them. In high context cultures and here in the United States, this takes you out of your "control" state, which is humiliating and lethal. Therefore, regardless, if you are told it will be another 15 or 20 minutes, please resist the urge to "sit down and make yourself comfortable" along with the rest of your competition. Please consider the additional nuance standing will provide. If you do sit down, get comfortable, take out your papers and your cell phone and your Blackberry and begin to multitask, what will happen when your escort or host arrives? You will need to jump to your feet and be ready to move in just a few seconds. You will need to hurriedly gather your belongings, stuff them all back into your bag quickly, and generally regain your composure and "control." Sitting, then, is a grave mistake. Sitting not only does not present a positive first impression of confidence and control, but also causes you to lose the momentum of having made good eye contact with your host as you greet and shake hands. Instead, you have shown you are not ready. You have allowed your client to see you in a less-than-ready state and you are vulnerable, not in control. You are already off to a poor start, indeed. And you thought you were there to take this important meeting? Use this waiting time to simply wait, in a poised, altogether, and ready state. When your escort or host arrives, you will be confident, in control, professional, and at the ready. Perception *is* reality.

Question: When departing the reception area with your host or escort, who leads?

Answer: Your host.

This is true even when the guest is a woman and the host is a man. There are no gender etiquette requirements in business. Also, your host knows the way!

This said, there is often some anxiety surrounding who should lead and who follows. Your goal as host is to place your guest at ease. Your role as guest is to defer to your host, who knows the way. If you are the host, tap a nuance to smooth the moment. Say: "Why don't I ask you to please follow me and I will direct you to my office." If you are the guest, say "Thank you, I am happy to follow your lead." Let the other person know that you (both) know the rules and your knowledge of etiquette will help put each of you at ease.

While en route to the meeting room, avoid awkward silences, which only serve to make others uncomfortable; make the effort to engage in small talk. Almost anything from the traffic, to directions, to the weather is appropriate on-topic material for small talk, as well as commenting on an unusual lapel pin or cuff links the other person is wearing, the office location, or the building itself. Ask open-ended questions that allow for free-flowing answers and conversation. Stay away from business topics. This is a small talk moment, an opportunity to gather valuable information about the other person by simply listening to her voice, hearing her talk, prior to the actual meeting. This is also a time to establish a connection and build trust by talking about nonbusiness topics.

Question: When you arrive in the meeting room, where do you sit?

Answer: Seating and where you sit in a meeting room is subtly yet very powerfully, significant, and there are several points of etiquette and protocol to consider, depending upon your host and your meeting location.

When the Meeting Is in Their Office

The number one rule regarding sitting when in the presence of your host is: always allow your host to be seated first in the courtroom. If you are permitted the luxury of selecting your own chair, when possible, choose the chair that is at an angle to your host, rather than across the desk, thereby eliminating the desk as barrier to growing the relationship. Also, if you have a choice, select the least comfortable chair. If you are comfortably seated in a plush leather chair, you tend to get a bit too relaxed and comfortable. Also, your energy level tends to drop off and your professional image will suffer. A less comfortable chair will encourage you to sit up, focus forward, and project energy. Remember, you are not there to get comfortable and have a relaxing conversation. You are there to project your best possible professional business image.

Approach the chair and pivot, letting the backs of your legs touch it before sitting down. This avoids the pratfall of missing the seat which may not happen often, but when it does, is humiliating. Take precautions. Sit two-thirds of the way back in the chair, versus on the edge, appearing that you might fly out, or sitting way back, which encourages one to slump. Sitting two-thirds of the way back in the chair creates a V between your back and the back of the chair. This positioning signals your connection to the other person, your desire to focus all your attention on them and conduct business.

Keep feet on the floor. If you cross your legs, soles should face the floor. This is important to keep the soles from showing because in some cultures, displaying the soles of one's feet is considered highly insulting. The soles of the feet are considered the lowest form of the body throughout Asia, Latin America, Arab countries, and Europe. Remember when they took down the Sadam Hussein statue? On the front page of every newspaper in the country, the photos depicted the people wacking the statue with the soles of their shoes—the ultimate insult. Therefore, to expose the soles of the feet, however inadvertently, might be misinterpreted. While you may not believe you will encounter this level of culture clash in your everyday meetings, it is certainly possible. We are global and live in a global, multicultural society. Better to err on the side of caution and be conservative and respectful. Train yourself to avoid the comfortable ankle-on-the-knee position in a business meeting, which also suggests via body language that you are "lower body closed." Save this casual, common North American sitting position for the comfort of your own home. If ladies cross, do so at the ankle or at the knees; however, remember to slope to either side.

When the Meeting Is in a Conference Room

If your meeting is in a conference room or the boardroom, you have an entirely different set of seating considerations. It is possible your host may have preplanned seating arrangements. If so, take your assigned seat. However, many people fail to take the lead on seating arrangements, and that leaves an opening for you to take a powerful position. If, when you arrive at the conference room your host invites you to "sit anywhere," as many do, this is your cue to make the most of the seating opportunity. Take the power seat in the conference room: the one facing the door. This gives you optimum viewing of those entering and exiting, as well as the full view of the table and players. Sitting here, at the head of the table, places you in the power position to in fact control the room. This seating choice, as with many astute tactics of the savvy business professional, has its roots steeped in history. The first and one of the most famous churches ever built in the United States is the First Baptist Church in Providence, Rhode Island. Typically, churches are built so that the priest faces the doors. However, because the priest's attention and focus is on the mass and not on who may be entering the church, this church was built so that the congregation's chairs faced the doors in order to have full view and to keep a watchful eye out for Indians approaching.

The Person of Honor is always seated to the host's right, per biblical tradition. If you are copresenting, have your copresenter sit across from you at the table instead of next to you. This way, the two of you can effectively communicate via eye contact and body language and together control the room during the course of your presentation. If your host does not step up, this is an opportunity for you to demonstrate your professionalism and exude confidence and authority in this meeting. Consider this chance to control seating arrangements, and thereby the room, as an opportunity to demonstrate your leadership style and communication skills. Take the power position and go!

Before everyone takes their seat, it is often a good time to approach each individual in the room, shake hands, provide introductions, and exchange business cards. If possible, collect the business cards of all present and then keep them with you. Subtly arrange cards around your portfolio in the order of where they sit, so you can easily refer to them during the course of the meeting and use individuals' names when addressing them. This will allow you to respectfully refer to people by name and keep control of the meeting. Also, with cards at the ready, you can accurately refer to each individual and her area of expertise as necessary.

When you begin the meeting and address business colleagues, consider standing. This is somewhat unusual in our country and you may feel a bit awkward at first. However, standing makes a powerful statement and has a tremendous impact. Your presence will dominate the room. I have been the only person to stand when addressing a meeting and individuals have commented at what a strong impression a simple gesture, such as standing, made. Standing, whether it is your meeting or if you have been asked to introduce yourself around the table, distinguishes you. This is a small nuance that sets you apart and helps distinguish you professionally. Also, whether standing or sitting, be sure to introduce yourself with energy and clarity. You have worked too hard to get this meeting and to begin your self-introduction with, "Hi guys, I'm Judy." This completely undermines your professional credibility. Instead, inject an energetic force into your greeting and tag line: "Hello! My name is Judy Bowman, founder of Protocol Consultants International. I am grateful to Messrs. Jones, Smith, and Anderson for inviting me to join you here at XYZ Company today to discuss our specialty of expertise, professional presence, and ways in which professionals can further distinguish themselves in business. I am honored to be with you here, this morning. Thank you!"

Be sure you have your tag line prepared—it's the one line that encapsulates who you are and what you can do for them.

What tools should you have in the meeting? There are several important elements to consider. Of course, bring plenty of business cards and corporate brochures, and provide an agenda. You can never be sure of how many unanticipated individuals may show up at your meeting and expect one. Have more than you believe you will need and have them in a readily accessible place, such as your portfolio. In this situation, it would be appropriate to use your quality business card holder, kept in your briefcase. Either way, business cards should be easily accessible.

Pack Efficiently, Travel Lightly

Question: What is the perception if you call on me carrying your largest briefcase?

Answer: This suggests that this meeting is one of many this day, or this week, rather than making the client feel special. Try to have two or more professional, quality briefcases: a small and a large, or a small, a medium, and a large, and use accordingly.

Have your quality professional portfolio. Freshen this with a new writing tablet and use quality pens; leave the Bics behind! This portfolio is an important visual for you. Like a briefcase, it says: This meeting is my number one priority. If you arrive at a meeting with a huge notebook full of information from other clients and other meetings, this client believes he is simply one of many you are juggling today. A slim portfolio and a clean pad convey focus: you are my one and only priority at this moment.

Before you open your portfolio, consider this nuance: Ask permission to take notes. Assume nothing in the relationship-building process. Earn the right to advance. Of course no one expects you to remember everything that transpires during the course of a meeting; in fact, you are expected to take notes. However, by asking, you have conveyed an extra measure of respect and deferred to your host's lead in a most polite and respectful way. This is a small gesture that goes a long way in terms of setting you apart.

Many people use visual aids, including a white board, an easel and pad, or even a computer and PowerPoint presentation. Whatever your visual aid may be, be sure it does not detract from you and your spoken message. The focus should be you. Visual aids should be considered as little more than props. Make sure you stand to the left of any materials, which helps keep the focus on you. Also, resist the urge to read your presentation. There is nothing more insulting than the presenter who reads her slides, especially word for word. Remember, your visual aids should serve only in support of you in your starring role. Keep the meeting upbeat, engaging, interactive, and professional. The focus: *you*!

Suppose you are offered coffee? Tea? Pastries? My advice: politely decline. While it is hospitable to offer guests a refreshment, remember: you are not there to eat. Also remember that most are nervous or anxious. Nerves may betray you and you do not want to be the individual remembered for spilling coffee all over the conference table or the person with croissant flakes on her lapel. Food and beverages can be disastrous and should be avoided. Exception: if it is clear to you that someone has gone to considerable time, effort, and trouble to have your favorite orange cranberry low-fat muffin available. In this case, it would be rude not to accept this; however, simply pick at it. Be careful eating and drinking at a business meeting, especially with important documents on the table. And finally, there is the image you portray when you dive in and take the last donut. Because you endeavor to project the most poised and professional, businesslike demeanor, digging through a tray of donuts to find the honey-glazed cruller will not enhance your professional image. This simply tells the room you are ravenous, or that you cannot resist a good donut. And, whatever you do, don't take the last donut!

When beginning your meeting, do a time check. State what topics you will cover within a specific time frame. State the current time and the time you expect the meeting to conclude. Let people know if there will be time for questions and answers at the conclusion.

Have a printed agenda for the meeting and distribute copies in advance. This always serves to help enhance your professionalism, as well as your attention to the big picture and small details. When I was in Beijing, I found it challenging to make these preparations. I had to go to the hotel's business center, where the machinery was unfamiliar to me. However, when I arrived at my meeting the next day and distributed my agenda, many at the meeting commented on the fact that I even had a printed agenda. This nuance was definitely noticed in a most favorable light. I was regarded as highly professional and this helped begin our meeting on a positive note.

Be sure to thank your host at the top of your presentation.

Question: Suppose someone arrives late to your meeting? Should you recap?

Answer: This is a delicate situation. While you want all the participants to be on the same page, with the same information, you do not want to punish the participants who arrived on time for the same meeting by making them sit through a dull recap of what they have already heard. The decision then rests on the rank of the person who has arrived late, together with just how late he is. Should the company president, for example, arrive late, it makes business sense to recap the meeting for this individual. Clearly, the company president will have significant impact on the outcome of this meeting and will need all relevant information to make an informed decision. However, this same individual may respectfully defer and suggest you continue on course, letting you know to find them later, to be brought up to date, before making final decisions.

If the individual who arrives late is a lower-ranking individual, it may simply be enough to make eye contact, hand that person an agenda, and give a one-line courtesy update of what you have just covered and where you now are, without interrupting the discourse of the meeting.

It also depends, of course, upon how late the latecomer is. A few minutes? Go ahead and recap. Half an hour? Perhaps. An hour? Rules of rank apply.

Question: Suppose you need to leave the meeting early. What should you do?

Answer: Alert the individual running the meeting ahead of time. Therefore, when you leave the presenter is not insulted or surprised in any way.

If you are presenting to a potential new client, remember to ask for the business at the conclusion of the meeting. Many people forget the ask, or are simply not geared up to do this. Please know this is a critical step toward moving from meeting to client relationship. You never want to leave a presentation meeting wondering: Did they like what they heard? Does it make sense to do business with me? Ask for the business.

When leaving, shake hands with all meeting participants once again and walk with them to the door. This period of post-meeting chat is often critical. During these relaxed, informal minutes is the time when real talk may actually develop. Don't run for the elevator. Walk with the others and engage them. This may be the moment in which you can make your greatest impact.

WHAT TO DO IF...

...someone barges into your meeting already in progress.

This depends on who the person is and how late she is. However, generally speaking, a more senior ranking individual should, respectfully, be provided with a brief recap upon arrival.

MEETING TIPS

- When possible, take the power seat. This will give you an edge, whether you are the host or the visitor.
- Decline hospitality. Nothing is gained if you spill coffee or toss crumbs on your lap. Better to say, "No, thank you." If it seems as though that might offend your host, take something small and let it sit.
- Investing in quality pens and other portfolios. School composition notebooks and fluorescent pens do not enhance your image at a meeting.
- Bring the smallest possible briefcase. A big one makes your client feel like one among way too many.
- Turn off your cell phone. Do this as you enter the client's property.
- Prepare and bring copies of an agenda. This is a way to have the meeting move ahead on your terms.
- Collect business cards and keep them in view. If you pocket the cards, you will be unable to refer to them during the meeting. By keeping them in view, you can use the names of the meeting participants. You can

also imply that you are keeping them close rather than "discarding" them in your briefcase.

- Keep your hands in view. Be aboveboard, rather than underhanded.

- Watch the clock. As with a presentation, time is of the essence. Stay with your originally stated time and stay on course.

- Use props judiciously. Even with high-tech items such as PowerPoint, the focus of the meeting should be on you and what you have to say. Do not let your props upstage you.

10

Gender Issues

A man and woman are seated in an office chatting before the start of a business meeting. An executive of the firm enters the office and approaches them to shake hands.

Question: What should the woman do?

Answer: She also stands to shakes hands.

When it comes to social graces, there are still many gentlemen and ladies who will act upon the wonderful traditional rules of social etiquette. However, when it comes to business etiquette, there are no gender differences. The same etiquette and protocol rules govern correct behavior for men and women in the business environment. This includes everything from shaking hands to standing, sitting, greetings, and introductions, opening doors, handling the check in a restaurant, helping another with coats, kissing, embracing, and attire. Rules that apply to men also apply to women. There is no gender split in the business arena.

Still, what sounds so simple can actually be quite vexing for the etiquette-conscious business individual. As we endeavor to show respect and deference to our clients and valued

152

business partners, we may struggle with the knowledge we have of social etiquette and the appropriate times to forgo those rules in favor of a gender-neutral stance. In this chapter, I will review several common situations that any business professional, a man or a woman, may encounter regarding gender issues and business etiquette.

The Door

Question: Who enters first?

Answer: Social etiquette suggests that gentlemen should hold the door open for women and permit them to pass through first. However, today, in a business situation, one's actions should be driven not by gender, but rather, by concerns regarding who is the host, client, or vendor will drive conduct in a business situation. This said, common courtesies should prevail. Whoever enters the door first is responsible for opening and holding it for the next person.

If you are with a client, regardless of gender, you should always defer to your client and show the greatest possible respect in every action, including passing through a door, entering a revolving door, helping another on and off with his or her coat, opening a car door, and permitting another to proceed or suggesting you lead, if you are in your office environment. It is appropriate then, regardless of your gender, to hold the door for your male or female client and acknowledge the gesture. Say, "Please, after you." (This is a nice nuance to say as you hold the door.) Remember, this is not a gender issue but a matter of displaying respect for your guest or client. I have found that this small nuance, this gesture, as a show of respect, is very much appreciated by both men and women.

Suppose one of your more traditional gentleman clients says, "Oh no, Judy, I insist, after you." The rule is after one attempt, accept the gesture and proceed. Having a debate with your client over the etiquette of doorway entry is certainly not your goal. The awareness of a gentleman's gesture, however, is duly noted and appreciated by most women. Getting through the door and down to business should be your focus. Therefore, do not stand in the doorway and continue the debate. After one attempt at deference, graciously accept the gesture and pass through.

Revolving doors present another consideration that should be addressed. Socially, it is appropriate etiquette for a gentleman to defer to the woman to proceed first through any door, including an automatically revolving door. And so, if the revolving door is automatic, the gentleman would naturally permit the woman to pass through first. However, automatically revolving doors are typically quite heavy, and so it would be appropriate for the gentleman to acknowledge the fact that the door is heavy and say, "This is a heavy door. Why don't I go ahead and push the door for you." Alternatively, some gentlemen will actually give a push to get the door started, let the woman enter the revolving door and then enter and push himself from behind her. Doing so is appropriate in a business setting, and the nuance in articulating the gesture is courteous. Some woman today, may take issue with this thinking, "That's ridiculous. I can certainly push my own door." However, the key is to remember the spirit in which the gesture is intended. Of course we can all open our own doors. Men and women, able bodied, are certainly perfectly capable of handling their own door. The gesture, however, from the gentleman, is intended as a mark of respect and no insult is intended. When a door is held, or an offer of assistance made, women should accept this in the spirit in which it is offered. This is another reason to articulate your gesture as you execute. If you say, "Allow me" in a tone of authority, warmth, and respect, you run far less risk of offending anyone.

Follow this same form when it comes to helping a man or woman on or off with his or her coat. Whatever gender, it is appropriate to offer to help the other individual on and off with his coat. Again, you are not suggesting the person is unable to manage her own coat. Rather, this is a small but gracious gesture, a show of respect.

Who should initiate a handshake? In business, there are no gender rules, once again. Socially, a gentleman typically defers to the woman's cue; however, in business, whoever initiates the handshake (thumb up, lean in, eyes forward—firm, one to two pumps, but not a bone-crushing grip) is making the power move in the relationship. Both men and women should use a handshake as a tool to affix and maintain control in business greetings and farewells, and when sealing a deal. Remember, your goal is to be a man/woman well met. You want to shake hands like you mean it, like you want to be remembered positively. Regardless of gender, initiate the handshake and be a person well met.

Seating presents another round of etiquette issues with gender overtones.

Question: Who is seated first?

Answer: You are present in a business, not a social gathering, and so your actions should be guided by business, not social, etiquette. Business etiquette suggests the host is always seated first at any business meeting. This is true regardless of the gender of everyone present. At a business dinner function, for example, it is the host, once again regardless of gender, who acts first to set the tone regarding sitting, toasting, napkin etiquette, initiating each course, and so on. When ordering, it is the person of honor, always seated to the host's right, who always orders first, regardless of gender.

When a woman excuses herself from the dining table, for whatever reason, social etiquette suggests gentlemen rise, out of respect, from their seats.

Question: Should this be done at a business dinner as well?

Answer: A business dinner is a social environment. Gentlemen should stand. These timeless, traditional shows of good manners and respect are yet another opportunity where one can distinguish one's self through actions.

Suppose a woman excuses herself from the dining table but the gentleman host and perhaps even her spouse/significant other do not rise.

Question: Should other gentleman at the table rise and risk upstaging, and possibly embarrassing, the host and even the spouse?

Answer: It is important to remember that this is a business gathering and so up-staging your host is not advisable. However, you want to maintain your own standards and show respect toward the woman excusing herself.

Alternative: You may consider what many men do: the half-rise, just a bit out of your seat. Make eye contact with the woman to complete the gesture. This half-rise conveys respect and allows you to maintain your high standards without disparaging the gentleman host or other men at the table.

Attire and Gender Issues

Many questions pertain to the differences in attire between men and women in the business world. It is believe that men have fewer choices. Conservative business dress directs them to the rather limited array of classic black, dark charcoals, and navy blues that dominate the business professional's wardrobe. Women are offered a much wider array of colors and styles. The fashion industry has been prolific in generating dozens of new takes on fashion statements women may wear, however not in a business setting.

My advice: To achieve the most professional image, women should defer to the four aforementioned basic suit colors. Even though you have been fashion advised of your "season" and even though you may look great in the fabulous fuschias or eggplants. When attending a business meeting, particularly a meeting with a first-time client, men and women should always defer to classic, conservative, quality-never-wrong business professional attire style and colors.

Even though you have been advised that your best color is red or blue, brown or lavender, please remember, you are not in a setting where your best colors are your best asset. Your purpose is business. Your goal is to project professional. Your asset is wearing power professional. You are endeavoring to portray a professional, polished image and want to make a connection. You are working to build a long-standing business bond with another business professional. Wearing a pretty pink outfit will not help your efforts. How you look is at issue. The colors you choose and wear are important toward that end. Let everything about you speak of professionalism. You want the focus regarding what you wear to be about business, not the latest fashion color or statement. Save your best colors for social gatherings, when you want all eyes to notice how great you look in green. In a business setting, keep the focus on the business, not fashion forward anything.

Shoes: No open toes, no sling backs. Shoes should always be darker than your hemline. White is taboo; off-white is fine. Spectators are fabulous. Suede is a notch above leather and no more expensive.

Keep makeup, jewelry, and fragrances at a minimum. Generally speaking, less is more. You do not want to go into a business setting streaked with war paint. This will not enhance your professional image or speak to your professionalism. Some jewelry is good. If even a small, simple gold or diamond stud on the ears, it is something that speaks to your attention to detail, being "finished" and put together. Put something on your lips. Lip glosses are terrific moisturizers and add something of detail about you. Similarly, wear something around your neck. A strand of gold or pearls, a pendant, anything that again speaks to your attention to detail about you.

The same is true for hair color and style. You may have gorgeous, long-flowing, fabulous locks; however, putting them on display in business will detract from your business mission. You don't want people looking at your beautiful golden locks or your roots. Gentlemen: Throw away the shoe polish you put on your hair; it is really obvious. You want colleagues to focus on your fabulous ideas. If you ladies have not had your hair cut in years it may be time to consider a classic blunt hair cut, which speaks volumes about you and your new professional image.

When it comes to manicures, stay with pale colors, pinks, corals, or neutrals. The French manicure is fabulous. Save any bright color for social occasions.

A final note: Never apply lipstick (or gentlemen, lip balm) at the dining room or meeting room table. A quick flick of the comb or brush in public for men or women is entirely inappropriate and unprofessional.

Skirts are still considered more professional than pants. Even then, the pantsuit is preferred. Always make sure your skirt is just above, at, or below the knee. There is merit to the thought the more professional the woman, the longer her hemline. Short, tight skirts in business completely undermine a woman's professional credibility and image. Wearing them is a form of self-sabotage in business.

Ruffles, lace, and cleavage and lace are strictly taboo in business, for the same reasons.

What to do with accessories? Purses never go on the table nor should they dangle from the back of the chair. Purses, if used at all, belong on the floor, or behind you on the seat, if in a restaurant. (The former is preferred.)

Briefcases should be quality, and the size briefcase should be determined by and tailored to the client and your presentation.

Often issues such as attire for men and women are driven by the company's culture. It is important to know your corporate audience and their view regarding gender issues. This will help you tailor your own presentation and foster a stronger connection.

Personal Contact

Another area where gender issues may arise comes when considering personal contact. We have already addressed the handshake. Both men and women can and should initiate the handshake. This is considered a power move in business introductions, greetings, and farewells, and the savvy business professional should utilize this important tool. However, there are other forms of greetings that need to be addressed.

Question: Is kissing, hugging, or embracing appropriate in business?

Answer: Kissing, as we know it here in North America, is generally discouraged in business. However, kissing and embracing is considered correct behavior and appropriate protocol in different parts of the world. For example, in Latin and Arab countries, touching, kissing, and embracing are appropriate. Personal space is virtually nonexistent. Even in the United States, presumably during the process of cultivating new relationships, individuals come to a new level. At this level, when professionals greet each other, kissing does happen. Remember once again, our goal is to grow the relationship. Therefore, if you have been successful in growing the relationship to the point where, when you meet and greet your client, and he approaches you with body language suggesting he is going in for the kiss, the hug, or the embrace, what are you going to do? Push him away? Certainly not. If the body language you are reading suggests he is coming in for the kiss, the hug, the embrace, then, go for it! However, if you are going to kiss someone, then kiss him on the cheek. Kiss right side to right side (reference, the handshake) and no air-kissing, which is interpreted as insincerity. If you are going to kiss, kiss cheek to cheek.

What is important here is never kiss publicly, such as in the meeting room. Rather, as you greet someone in the lobby, or in your office, you may give them a warm and sincere greeting by way of kiss or hug, discreetly.

More and more, because I believe we are global and, constantly learning from and adapting to each other's ways and traditions, we see more people greeting and saying farewell with the French, kissing on either cheek. There were several fun photos in major newspaper publications recently depicting President Bush kissing Condoleezza Rice. Six or eight frames, and he might miss and get her nose or her teeth! Be careful when you go in for the second cheek. It can be missed and awkward!

Aside from cultural differences, it is important to be aware of personalizing individual aspects of any given client relationship. If your client is a kissy/huggy person and he or she approaches you to kiss, big hug, or offer an embrace, you certainly cannot push him or her away. Generally speaking, kissing, hugging, touching, and extending compliments are delicate territory; sexual harassment issues are real today and you certainly do not want to risk offending anyone. That said, your goal in growing the relationship is to get to the kiss, hug, or embrace phase. These are the signs you are building and nurturing a true bond.

In business, people develop relationships where a kiss and embrace are natural. The bottom line here is that if you have the relationship and want to kiss, you should do so, but not in the boardroom or any other public, professional forum. If you kiss, kiss away from public scrutiny.

Additionally, I believe the events of September 11th, which have changed our lives forever, may have something to do with this. People today value and appreciate people and friendships more than ever. Generally speaking, we as a society endeavor to travel less and try to enjoy time being at home with friends and family more. When we care for someone, it is natural to express our feelings. Kisses and hugs are such forms of expression.

That said, discretion is still key. Suppose you are dating someone within your company? We spend more hours at work than we do at home, and it is not uncommon to have personal relationships evolve from daily workplace contact. Many men and women have met their spouses through business. However, while this is quite common, it is important to keep intimate personal contact that comes with a personal relationship separate. This clearly suggests no hugging and kissing. However, this also extends to looks and glances and other forms of flirtation that are quite lovely in their proper place but are most unwelcome in a business environment.

How should you handle a situation in which a client or guest invades your personal space? Please know that personal space, that area around you that provides a comfort zone, varies from country to country. Animals have it—it is called the circle of trust—should anyone permeate their circle, they will instinctively pull away. Touching an arm or leg or simply being closer than one would prefer? Women may find this happens for a variety of reasons. This may be a cultural misunderstanding. In some cultures, Latin and Arab countries for example, it is perfectly acceptable for a man to freely and deliberately touch a woman on the arm or leg and violate all personal space as we know it. However, this does not suggest a woman must conform to this in a business environment. You might consider using some humor to diffuse any misunderstanding while connecting and explaining that in America, it is considered customary to put a bit more distance and touching is typically taboo. Ultimately, you will be respected for this.

The reason may not be cultural. The person may be testing you to see how you will react. Or, this may be a genuine case of an inappropriate advance and sexual harassment. It is reasonable for a woman to speak up and defend herself against such unwanted attentions. The use of humor may help you make your point without disrupting the business function of the gathering. Your goal is to keep everyone on a smooth playing field.

In a recent interview with Candance O'Terry, Founder of Exeptional Women and President of American Women in Radio and Television, I was asked how I would define a successful woman, which I would like to share with you.

I define a successful woman as one who knows she is a woman. She should use her talents, personality, looks, charm, and powers of persuasion to her advantage, as men always have. Because most women are, by nature, nurturers, they are accustomed to caring for others. They need to be reminded to use their innate powers and get to "the ask."

Finally, a successful woman is one who is confident in herself, enough to extend herself and help other women. A successful woman will embrace and help other women achieve, and a victory for me is a victory for all!

TIPS ON GENDER ISSUES

- Lipstick (ladies) and lip balm (gentlemen) should never be applied in public.
- Purses, small, if even required, are never placed on the table in the dining or meeting room and are never flung across the back of the chair.
- Personal hygiene: running a quick comb or brush through your hair in public: jamais!
- Ladies who are entering and exiting a car: Sit down, knees together, and swing legs together into the car. Reverse the process to exit.

- Removing one's coat: Start from the bottom button and work your way up.

- Ladies may sit at a table and drop their coats off the shoulders and rest along the top of the chair back, if no coat check is available. If crossing legs, ladies should remember to slope to the right or to the left, from the knees or ankle, calves should slope. The nuance and the difference is truly remarkable.

- Always carry an extra pair of hose.

- Men and women should have regular manicures.

- Clip facial hair, nose and ear hair, and check bushy eyebrows.

- French cuffs are fabulous for both men and women. Plus, the cuff link can be a great lead in for conversation.

- Less is more with respect to fragrances, jewelry, accessories, and makeup.

- Attire: Think investment dressing, quality, classic, and conservative.

11

Attire

Question: You are preparing to dress for a client presentation where you will be meeting with various levels of executives, including the company president. You have three suits from which to choose: black double-breasted, shark's skin gray, and navy blue. Your client is a major insurance company. Which suit do you choose?

Answer: Take your cue from the company's culture and discipline. This is an insurance company; therefore, go conservative. Save your fashionable, double-breasted suit for coming off your yacht and your shark's skin gray suit for Las Vegas. The classic navy blue suit is never wrong.

Attire is a critical tool in business that is far too often overlooked. Professional business dress is not simply a matter of personal taste or even fashion. How you dress in a business environment is also a means of communicating with your client. It speaks volumes about you. Does everything about you speak of quality? Are you dressed in appropriate business colors? Are your accessories conservative and understated? Are your shoes classic, polished, and professional? All these elements factor into the overall first impression you will make when meeting with your clients. You may be a very fashionable person socially, with exquisite taste and a flair for the latest look. This is useful in your social life. However, when it comes to proper attire in business, rules apply. Remember, these guidelines are designed to help advance, not to make decisions regarding professional business attire.

Men's Attire

Contrary to popular belief, men have many important choices to make when it comes to professionanl business attire. There are many opportunities to shine and just as many ways to make professional business attire faux pas.

Suits

What are the possible color choices? Navy blue, navy blue, and navy blue. I am just kidding! However, navy blue, rather than royal blue or power blue, is a fail-safe choice for suit colors. Others such as black, charcoal, and pinstripe in these colors are also appropriate for a traditional business suit. Are any other colors acceptable in business? In warm temperatures, a younger gentleman may get away with seersucker; however, this is a risk. Seersucker is a fabric that suggests social rather than business environments. Other light colors such as off-white and khaki, but not pastels, may also be considered in tropical climates. Brown is absolutely out as a business suit color. Brown is considered dull and its wearer duller. Do not even think about wearing brown in business.

For any first time meeting, the wisest choice is the conservative one. Dark-colored suits are always appropriate in a business setting, and always in the evening. Anyone wearing a light-colored suit to an evening function will stand out in quite an unfavorable way.

When it comes to suit style, double-breasted is considered too fashion forward for the business meeting. Save this for a social outing or to wear with a quite established client relationship. Three-button suits are the appropriate choice for a business occasion. The top two buttons should be buttoned, the bottom button open to vent for men and women. The single vent in the back is considered most professional. The flap back is second. Body type will also drive which back men should wear.

Lapels

Men's lapels should not be too wide or too narrow. Find a moderate, classic width that works.

Question: Is it ever appropriate to remove one's suit jacket at a business event?

Answer: Generally speaking, the jacket should stay on. One exception: If the host removes his jacket, this is a silent signal that others may do the same. However, it is not required and it is still more appropriate to keep one's jacket on. In very warm conditions, it may also be appropriate to shed one's jacket; however, keep in mind what your shirt most likely looks like underneath. Will that image of you in a damp and wrinkled shirt enhance your business image and build trust with your client? Most likely, not. It may be worth the discomfort to keep your jacket on. Cuffed pants are appropriate in a business as they suggest a more finished look. However, a cuffed pant is best suited for a certain body type. A shorter, stouter gentleman should generally not wear cuffed pants, because they will not flatter his body type.

Shirts

When it comes to shirts, men should opt for white or light blue. The power stripe is also acceptable. There was a time when ecru was considered an appropriate color for men's shirts, but no longer. Make sure your shirt collar flatters your face and jowls. If you are not certain, ask the advice of a personal shopper at almost any department store. This is the portion of your attire that frames your face. Make the choice that best sets off your best look. Also, make sure the collar fits. Shirt collars that are too large suggest you have either been quite ill, lost weight, or are weak. A strong look requires a tight collar. Button-down collars suggest a more casual, preppy look. There is the British tab collar, which is fabulous. Using collar stays is helpful. Shirt cuffs, particularly with French cuffs, should extend one-quarter inch beyond the jacket sleeve. The white collar shirt or the "Wall Street shirt" is a fabulous look, but it is not considered a conservative look. One must "earn the right to wear" this in some businesses, such as the financial services industry. A new intern sporting a white collar/blue shirt/French cuff shirt will most likely be mocked. As with comfortable, soft, Italian tassel loafers, one needs to earn the right to wear this look in business.

Ties

Ties are perhaps one accessory with which men can express their individual style. People notice the tie a man wears. It is considered a reflection of his personality. Still, it is critical to remain within the bounds of professional, conservative taste, and quality when choosing this particular piece of attire. Conservative ties are always appropriate and never wrong. Stay away from obnoxious oranges; loud, gaudy reds; paisleys; and large polka dots. They will not enhance your professional image.

Tie tips

☞ The color blue engenders trust.

☞ Forest green signifies friendship.

☞ Black-and-white ties suggest Las Vegas.

☞ Power ties come in rich red, light blue, or ice blue. Pink and yellow may also qualify, but these colors do not flatter all skin tones. Ask professional advice on this matter.

☞ Stripes, such as a tasteful combination of bur-
gundy and gold or green and blue, work well.

☞ If you have a spot on your tie, throw it out.

A fashion note: Cause-related ties, such as those connected
to a charity or arts event, are popular and not inappropriate.
They are often an excellent way to express your personality
and convey yet another dimension of you, your personality,
and your personal commitments. If you are aligned with or
committed to a particular charity or involved in a program
that has designed a tie as a charitable item, these are often
considered appropriate to wear in a business setting.

Tie pins, tie tacks, and gold tie ropes are functional and
fabulous accessories.

Shoes

The most classic and professional choice in shoe styles is
the presidential style with or without the cap toe. Choose black
rather than brown or cordovan. I once had the opportunity to
hear Sandy Weil of Citigroup address the issue of gentleman's
shoes. He himself was wearing brown leather Italian loafers
with tassels at the time. He was quoted in a major newspaper
the next day. Two paragraphs were devoted to what Mr. Weil
had to say about men's shoes. "Men should wear the black
presidential tie shoe," he said, "until they earn the right to
wear" these (Italian tassle loafers). I concur. Men of stature
and prominence may exercise some latitude in footwear. Those
on the way up should keep classic black close.

Socks

Men's socks should be thin, black, and executive length.
They should be tall and taut enough to cover your leg so that
your bare legs are not visible whether you are sitting or standing. Visible leg hair is tacky. Should the elastic in your socks
not be reliable, use gentlemen's braces. Rubber bands also

work. Socks can be a fashion statement for men today, and many men use socks like ties to express their personalities or passions. However, like brown Italian loafers, the "right to wear" funky socks must be earned.

Hats

Gentlemen remove hats indoors. At an outdoor café, the site is considered a restaurant, despite its lack of four walls, so that hat should come off. If you are an individual who is sensitive to sun or otherwise needs the hat for health reasons, that is an exception. However, sports hats such as baseball caps are not considered professional. Many gentlemen professionals have been seen shedding their baseball caps in favor of the fabulous fedora. This is a great, professional look.

Women's Attire

Suits

The skirt/dress suit is the most appropriate and business professional look for women; pantsuits are still number two. As is the case for men, the most appropriate suit colors for women are navy blue, black, dark gray, and pinstripe. This may seem surprising, given the full array of colors available to women in most department stores. However, when it comes to the business environment, women and men should opt for classic, conservative, never-wrong business professional colors.

I consulted for a company that was quite conservative in its culture. On my first day at the company headquarters, I opted to wear what I thought was a very professional, Chanel-style gold suit. It was a warm day and so I thought a light color would be appropriate. It was a beautiful suit and I felt I was appropriately dressed. Prior to starting my back-to-back sessions, I ran into the company president in the hall. We shook hands, exchanged greetings, and went on our ways. I conducted the morning session, and then, during our half-day break, the woman helping me coordinate our seminars shared with me the fact that the company president, whom I had met that morning, was concerned about my professional image. In the future, it was suggested to me, if I hoped to be invited back to work for this firm while on their company site, I should wear only the most professional color suits. The colors were spelled out for me: navy blue, black, charcoal gray, and pinstripe in any of these colors.

I was mortified. However, the experience was instructive. Amazingly, I still work for this firm! We all make mistakes and will continue to do so. Showing a sincere effort to rectify and remedy any situation will be appreciated in the spirit in which it is offered. Even when the suit is professional in design, it must also be professional in color. There may be occasions when a more colorful suit is appropriate, but not on the first meeting or initial presentation with a new client. Be sure your suit colors conform to the classic business palate.

While conservative colors for suits are the rule, this rule is also one which an individual can earn the right to break. I met with a woman recently, a very senior executive in her firm, who shared with me her story regarding professional attire. She was making a major key presentation to the president of her firm along with several of her high level peers. She woke up that morning and had to choose between a classic, never-wrong, quality black suit or pink. She opted for the pink. She gave her presentation, and following the presentation, met with the president, who gave her high marks on her presentation and made no mention of her pink suit.

My reaction: Clearly this woman had the stature and confidence to make this color choice and make it work. This worked for her because she knew the rules and yet made the conscious decision to break them for her own effect. However, as with Sandy Weil's Italian loafers, that right to break the rules has to be earned. In her position, she had the status and earned the right to make choices and break rules. I expect that on her way up the ladder in the company, this woman wore more black than pink. And, if she were making the presentation to outside clients instead of internal peers, her choice would most definitely have been black.

There are many wonderful colors in clothing. A woman may feel she looks best in an eggplant, lavender, tangerine. However, these are colors best suited to social environments. Your goal in business is to establish trust and grow the relationship. Impressing the other party with your fashion forward tastes is rarely on the agenda. Brown, as always, is considered strictly taboo, for women, too! Save your brown suits for social affairs or to wear, if at all, well after you have the client relationship.

Shirts

After your choice of suit color, your choice of shirt may well be the next most important item in your attire checklist. Neutrals are best. Your shirt, blouse, or sweater should not be too bulky or formfitting. The neck should not reveal cleavage. In Japan, the most sensual part of a woman's body is considered the neck, and so any "V" necklines would be considered taboo. Lace and ruffles are not considered appropriate in business. Toss anything even remotely worn looking. Natural fabrics such as cotton, silk, linen wool, and cashmere are best. In all clothing, choose quality fabrics.

Pants

Thanks largely to the fashion leadership of Senator Hilary Clinton, the pantsuit is more widely acceptable for women in business today. Senator Clinton is frequently photographed at professional events wearing a pantsuit. Notice that Senator Clinton conforms to the standards of business dress by choosing conservative colors such as black, blue, and gray. Her shirt is appropriate to the setting with a conservative neckline and an appropriate fit.

If you choose to wear pants, a pantsuit, rather than slacks and a jacket, is the best choice. The blazer look is considered more casual. Remember to button your jacket, leaving the bottom open, as men do. Make sure you know a good tailor and ensure clothes fit well. Also, understand what styles best flatter your body type. If you are unsure, enlist the assistance of an image consultant.

Hosiery

Whether it is 100 degrees or 100 degrees below zero, ladies hosiery is still appropriate leg wear for women in a business setting. Choosing the right color is important. White is reserved for nurses. White hose and white shoes are taboo in business. In warm summer months, choose neutral shades or beige. In transitional months, you may opt for tan. In colder months, black opaque is appropriate. A common hose error: Many women make the faux pas of wearing sheer black hose during the day. Sheer is reserved for evening and formal events. Instead, opaque is a more professional, and I believe flattering, choice in a business setting.

Shoes

Like the wonderful array of colors in the suit department, there is an amazing selection of shoes available to women today. Many women may be enticed to try more fashion forward footwear; however, this is a faux pas in business. Sling backs, open toes, and stilettos are out of place in the business world. Wearing them will not enhance your credibility. Instead, the best choice is the classic pump. Suede is a notch above leather in terms of favorable impression and it is no more expensive.

Will anyone really notice your shoes? Absolutely. This is especially true if you are making a presentation and stand in front of an audience on a stage or platform. The audience will have a direct eye line to your shoes. If your shoes are more appropriate for a party than a business function, they will notice. If they are worn, scuffed, or poorly maintained, they will notice. If they are not the right color to complement the rest of your professional attire, they will notice. Rule: Your shoes should be darker than your hemline. Your audience will check you out from head to toe. If you are appropriately attired, this will not faze you in the least. You will be confident because you will know you are perfectly, correctly, professionally attired.

Jewelry

When it comes to any accessory, less is more. Jewelry is appropriate to complement business attire provided it conforms to standards of conservative taste. Gold and pearls are considered the most classic choices. If silver favors your skin tone, hair, or eyes or other aspects of your attire, silver would be an acceptable choice. Overall, a good jewelry combination might consist of a watch, perhaps a bracelet, something around your neck (such as a gold chain, pearls, or small pendant) and earrings. Nothing that dangles should be worn. This applies to earrings and to bangle bracelets. They are wonderful accessories for social dress; however, they will detract from your professional image in a business setting.

Some women opt to wear a large pin to programs such as networking events. The thinking is this highly visible piece will help initiate conversation. Be careful about the prop you wear and where the conversation may lead. Your goal is to establish credibility and build trust with current and potential clients and business associates. A classic scarf is also a great accessory.

A word about watches: It was once considered a smart strategy to wear a very expensive watch in business. The inference being you are established and can afford such a watch. Brands such as Rolex became synonymous with success in the business world. Today, that idea has softened somewhat. Wearing a solid gold Rolex might be considered ostentatious. Conventional wisdom suggests only a small percentage of those who own the solid gold Rolex can truly afford it. In business today, this may be problematic if the person across the table from you does not have one because she could not afford such an expensive item. And you are soliciting them? It is far better to err on the side of conservative and wear one of your other quality, yet understated, timepieces. We further suggest saving your sports watches for when you are engaged in sporting activities. That said, if you are a serious athlete and wear a heart rate monitor because you compete in Iron Man, for example, then, this would certainly stimulate not only conversation, but lead to a better understanding about you as a person.

Scarves

A high-quality fashion scarf is an elegant accessory; however, it must be worn properly to achieve the desired effect. Any scarf that keeps trying to fall off is a hindrance and should be eliminated. Also, remember that a scarf may tend to make you feel warm. If you are likely to feel anxious, the scarf may add to the sensation that you are melting. Should this be the case, it makes sense to leave the scarf at home or take it off after you have extended welcome greetings and before you begin your presentation, regardless of how good it looks. Scarves are a great accessory. Think: classic names such as Burberry and Ferragamo, and subtle, classic prints. Learn how to tie them and avoid loud, screaming scarves, as with gentlemen's ties.

Purses

Like briefcases, it is better to carry a small purse rather than a large one to a business meeting. Those large leather handbags that serve us so well shopping are out of place in a business setting. They suggest, as does a large briefcase, that you have many other things to attend to and have a lot going on in your life with this huge bag slung over your shoulder. This is not appropriate in this business meeting to help enhance your professional image.

Choose a small purse that you can wear over your shoulder and forget about. Often, I carry a purse small enough to stash inside my briefcase, so it is never seen. Carry only the essentials in your purse. Items such as hair spray, dental floss, breath mints, lip gloss, and eyeliner are all important. Just be sure you choose sample sizes so that they can be carried discreetly.

Question: Where do purses belong during a meeting?

Answer: Inside the briefcase works for convenience and safekeeping. The other option is under the table by your feet. This applies in the meeting room or in a restaurant. Resist the urge to sling your purse over the back of your chair. This does not cast the favorable, professional image you wish to portray.

Fragrances

Fragrances follow the same general rules as jewelry and other accessories: Less is more. Indeed, I recommend avoiding fragrances all together. You can never be certain if a fragrance will offend or distract your business associate. However, if you must, be sure the fragrance is very light. An overpowering scent, no matter how attractive, will not enhance your professional image.

Attire Issues Affecting Both Men and Women

Coat Etiquette

There are two important issues to address with regard to coats. The first is what coat to choose and the second is how to handle the coat in a business setting.

First, coat choice. Opt for professional colors and styles. Ski parkas and other sporty coats are fine for weekends and social gatherings, but they will not enhance your image in a professional setting. Dark colors, or a khaki beige or green khaki color coat, convey the appropriate level of respect and professionalism. Be sure the length of your coat is longer than your hemline for women, and for men, mid-calf length is far more professional than above the knee. If your coat is worn, or frayed, replace it. If it is ill-fitting, have it tailored to fit. Make sure you dry clean if necessary. Be aware that your coat will be seen by your clients or business associates. If you take care to make sure your attire is perfectly correct, it would be a shame to wear a sloppy, inappropriate, ill-fitting or poorly maintained coat over your perfectly chosen suit. Your coat will be visible as you exit your car, enter the reception area, and walk into the office. Consider coats as seriously as you consider the rest of your attire.

There are several additional issues regarding coat etiquette. Socially, it is considered appropriate protocol for gentlemen to help a lady on and off with her coat. In the business world today, there are no gender splits when it comes to proper etiquette. Both men and women should adopt the gracious gesture of helping each other on and off with their coat. The gender of either party is not a factor in business. Rather, this is a gesture of respect that should be extended, regardless of gender. I have found in my experience that both men and women clients appreciate this gesture. Ideally, the person being helped with his or her coat should offer to reciprocate the gesture.

What about your coat in a restaurant? In the best case scenario the coat is checked at the coat check area. However, some restaurants do not have coat checks, and in some cases, you may not feel comfortable leaving your coat behind. If you do arrive at the table with your coat, the proper procedure is: Unbutton your overcoat, from the bottom button up. Sit down at the table, still wearing your coat. Then, once seated, let the coat slide off your shoulders and fall over the back of the chair. It is perfectly acceptable to dine and spend the entire event sitting on your coat in this fashion. Resist the urge to take off your coat and stash this on another chair at the table.

Gloves

Gloves come off when shaking hands. This is true even if you meet your client or business associate outside in the dead of winter and it is zero degrees. Off come the gloves for the handshake; Eliminate the barrier. You do not want anything to interfere with the personal connection you are endeavoring to establish. The only person technically permitted to shake hands with their gloves on is the Queen of England!

Business Casual

What is business casual? This question plagues many in the business world. Beginning in the 1990s, fueled in part by the youthful makeup of the dot-com business leaders, the trend away from traditional business attire took hold. Businesses began instituting "business casual" days. Often the phrase will appear on a meeting agenda or conference brochure. The reality is, nobody has really defined what business casual means. And, it means different things to different people and firms.

Does it mean khakis and a polo shirt? Can it mean sandals or jeans? No tie? No hose or socks? Fashion colors? Business casual can mean any, all, or none of these things. Business casual has no hard-and-fast definition.

As a result, if you are invited to an event and are informed this will be business casual, it would be wise to ask what this means as definitions vary widely from company to company. We have seen a return to business professional attire. Professionals dress professionally to convey respect, and inspire trust. Business casual has taken a back seat and is not prevalent in the highly competitive business world today.

Sunglasses

Wearing protective eyewear is appropriate when approaching or leaving your event or meeting; however, it should be removed as soon as you see the whites of their eyes in business. Sunglasses conceal the eyes, creating a barrier, not enabling direct eye contact to help establish trust to grow the relationship. Warm, direct eye contact is a must for creating a bond of trust between you and your business colleague. Be sure your sunglasses come off as soon as you meet/greet others and shake their hand.

Formal Events

Formal events call for a tuxedo for men and appropriate dress and accessories for women. Women should be aware that both the color and the fabric of the dress at a formal event should be considered. A black velvet dress, for example, is perfect for a fall or winter affair. However, the velvet would be out of place in warmer months. Choose both fabric and color with care. Sparkles are appropriate in the evening but not at an afternoon garden party; choose cotton, or linen during the warm summer months.

Holiday party attire

What to wear to the company holiday party? This is not as difficult a question as it seems. The reason is this: Although this is called a party, it is not. It is still work. You will see and be seen by your business associates, colleagues, senior managers, and clients. Therefore, your choice of attire is quite simple. It must be appropriate business dress.

There may be the temptation at a holiday party to let loose and show off your personal, more fashionable side. This is understandable. However, keep in mind that these are still the same people you will see after the New Year around the conference table, at the networking events, and in the halls of the company. Do not forsake your professional image for the sake of a party dress. Choose conservative attire for the holiday party. And let it set the tone for your behavior that evening: eat, drink (if at all), and party in moderation, with a conservative slant. Be sure your professional image is intact.

ATTIRE TIPS

- Choose dark, conservative suit colors. This applies to both men and women.
- Dress a notch up from your client as a gesture of respect, and maintaining professional standards.
- Business casual means different things to different companies. Ask if you do not know the company's specific rules.
- Keep accessories, including jewelry, fragrances, and scarves, at a minimum. Less is more.

- Helping another with his or her coat is a gesture of respect. Men and women can both offer and receive this gesture with equal positive impact.

- Avoid overly fashionable or alluring clothes. Save formfitting, bright colors and plunging necklines for social occasions.

- Shoes should be conservative: a presidential laced style for men, a classic pump for women. The "right to wear" footwear must be earned.

- Even business "parties" call for business conservative dress.

- The era of the solid gold Rolex is past. Choose a quality watch. No sports gear or kiddie designs.

Business Cards

Question: You are attending a business networking event and learn the CEO of a firm you have been targeting for months has shown up unexpectedly. You arrange to be introduced by a mutually respected third party and the CEO asks for your business card. You present it. Do you ask for his?

Answer: Absolutely not. Rule: Never ask a very high-ranking executive for his or her business card. Should you do this, however, be prepared to receive little more than a rather cold stare in return. While exchanging business cards at a networking event is expected and common practice among the rank and file of the business world, high-ranking executives will often carry and exchange cards only with those of similar status.

This chapter will explore the almost ritualistic world of business card exchange. Much of what we have learned about the protocol of business cards and their exchange comes to us from the Japanese. The literal translation is the Japanese word, *Makko* meaning "my face." The business card represents one's life and is an extension of one's life. Therefore, the quality paper stock is important; the almost ritualistic process and detailed procedures governing where the business card is kept, how the card is presented, acknowledged, used, and ultimately placed, is critical. There is much we can learn from our cross-cultural neighbors in this regard, specifically pertaining to their significance and, rules governing exchange. This remains an area where many finer points of etiquette are to be carefully considered, all out of respect. Understanding the undercurrents of business card exchange can give you a significant advantage during this very frequent and common moment of business practice.

Choosing Your Card

Business card protocol consideration begins long before exchange during a meeting or networking event. Indeed, the entire process begins with the very inception of the card itself. When crafting your business card, remember this piece of paper represents you. The business card is truly not just a piece of paper with your contact information. Rather, the business card is the physical manifestation of you and the firm you represent. With this is mind, choose your card wisely.

Begin with high-quality paper stock for the card itself, as close to 100% cotton stock as possible is recommended for the most quality, professional-looking business card. More business professionals are opting to have their business cards engraved, which may be a bit more costly but projects a rich, quality look.

When designing the layout of your card, be sure your name stands out. Format information so your name is prominent and not overwhelmed by lines of other information on the card such as telephone numbers and e-mail addresses and other data. Contact information is important, of course, but this card must deliver you first, above all, and then your contact information. Your name is the most important and should be the focal point on your business card.

Be sure the color of your card is businesslike and reflects your brand. White is the most common professional choice. Off-white or ecru is also rich, elegant, and professional. Avoid colors and pastels such as pink, lavender, or copper. These colors may distract from the professional image you strive to present. That said, if your business is one that uses color, perhaps as an artist or designer, then more liberal use of color and graphics may be in order. Similarly, if your business is one that involves children or toys, use of rainbow colors or other playful motifs may dovetail nicely with your brand and image. The key is to have your business card enhance and complement your image rather than distract or detract from it.

In some cases, creative design and enhancements on business cards can effectively be used to distinguish rank or status. I was at a networking event where I received six business cards from individuals with the same high-technology firm. Four of the cards were regular, white, high-quality cards. One had an elegant silver "thumbprint" in the upper corner of the card, and one card, clearly from an even more senior executive, had a gold "thumbprint," designating his rank/status within the firm. These cards were beautifully presented and the choice of gold and silver reflected appropriate designations of the individuals whose names they were on. Ultimately, the purpose of the business card is intended to reflect and represent you, your firm, and the quality your firm provides. Choose the card and design it with this objective in mind.

Using cheap materials in a business card can leave a lasting negative impression. I had a meeting with the president of a company and one of his managing directors from the same firm. The president's business card was quality stock and engraved. The card I received from his managing director was cheap and flimsy. It was laminated and the print and layout were poorly designed. The print was so small I had trouble reading it, even with my glasses on! This business card disconnect was what stood out in my mind. Why would the president invest in quality business cards for himself and not for one of his managing directors? Was this managing director not worthy of the investment of a quality business card? Did the president believe this was a detail that could be overlooked? That no one would really notice? It was not so much the fact that I was presented a flimsy card as it was the inconsistency and lack of attention to details that was pronounced in my mind. Either way, noticing the discrepancy and inconsistency damaged my impression of these gentlemen, their firm, the way they operate, and ultimately, our business relationship. I first had a poor first impression of the managing director. His card lacked quality and attention to details and inspired no confidence, which ultimately undermined my ability to respect or even trust him. It was as if he came to the meeting dressed in an obviously cheap suit or showed poor table manners at a lunch. How could I place my trust in this individual when he could not be bothered to attend to something so fundamental as to have professional business cards? Incidentally, he was wearing a rather cheap-looking suit. The perception was real.

At the same time, this gentleman's business card had a ripple effect on my impression of the president of the company. While the president's card was outstanding, I was not impressed that he did not deem his subordinate "business card worthy" and permitted him to represent himself and his firm with such a tacky, poor quality business card. Branding and internal consistency clearly are not important to the president of this firm. In what other ways might he be inattentive or inconsistent, and where else might he cut corners when he believes no one will notice?

Where to Keep Business Cards

We should all have our quality business card cases where business cards are kept in order to retain their perfect look.

Or, business cards may be kept in the envelope pocket of our portfolios. If networking, as we have suggested, business cards may be placed in pockets, one for incoming and one for outgoing cards. Some gentlemen keep them "at the ready" in their breast pocket. Business cards should not be kept in gentlemen's wallets, which are usually kept in back pockets and sat on, where the cards ultimately could get bent. Keep business cards perfect and clean. Toss any that have a frayed or bent edge or mark of any kind.

How to Present a Business Card

The most appropriate and correct way to present a business card comes to us from the Japanese. This formal, again almost ritualistic, process is one which conveys great respect. Hold the card, print side up, in both hands, with your thumb and forefinger carefully holding the two corners. Present the card forward so the receiver does not have to turn it around to read it. Present it in this manner with a bow-like gesture.

A less formal version of presenting a business card is to hold the card on one corner with your thumb and forefinger and present. Please know that if you see the card coming with a thumb in each corner, it is appropriate to receive in kind. Should the card be presented to you with a thumb in one corner, receive this similarly, in the same way, with a thumb on the opposite corner. Be careful thumbs do not conceal information on the card, thereby disrespecting one's life!

In North America, it is not uncommon to see business cards tossed about like toys. Many times, they are flung or shot across a conference table like a hockey puck, or handed to strangers with complete disregard for essential, required attention and ceremony. Casual treatment of your own business card devalues your own image. Remember, this is an extension of you and you are presenting yourself to someone with whom you hope to have a professional relationship. Treat your business card and your service or business with respect. This will help to enhance your image as one who is professional and respectful.

How to Receive a Card

Appropriate etiquette and protocols involved in receiving a business card are just as important as presenting one. Indeed, when you are presented with a business card in the appropriate manner, the correct way in which you receive this will certainly resonate with the giver. Clearly, the giver understands appropriate protocol. When you receive a business card properly, you send the signal that you also care about and know correct protocols and professional business conduct and behavior.

When you are presented a business card, accept it, look at it, and study it. Acknowledge the card. This simple act is significant. In fact, if you do not do all these steps, this will not help enhance your professional image.

Here is a story that illustrates my point. A friend told me about his first business trip to Hong Kong. As he was introduced to his potential new clients, he was given several business cards and he, as a matter of course, took each card with both hands and studied the card, really studied it for a while, looking back at the giver. Unbeknownst to him, this served to endear him completely to his potential new clients, and they developed a fantastic business and personal relationship. This act was done innocently but quite naturally, and his instincts served him well. Showing respect for another person and his business, which is what the business card represents, is significant and makes a powerfully strong statement about you.

How many times have we seen someone receive a business card and simply stash it into a wallet or drop it in a briefcase? This is a mistake and a missed opportunity to show respect and demonstrate that you know the difference.

Upon receiving a card, look at it, study it, read the name and title. Then, acknowledge the card by raising your eyes or eyebrows, making good eye contact with the individual presenting the card. This act of acknowledging the card—the quality, this individual, her life—is truly what the business card exchange process is all about. Please be acutely aware of the importance of truly *acknowledging* any business card you receive.

In addition, studying the card in this way provides you with the opportunity to make a visual connection with the name, so you are able to use it right away in conversation. Make an association to help remember the name. Receive the card and acknowledge its giver with expressive eye contact while showing you are impressed. It is also appropriate to extend a slight, most respectful bow.

Once you have received and read the business card, you will need to put it someplace. In a networking event, you may place the card in your jacket pocket. Indeed, it is wise to wear a jacket with two ample pockets to a networking event. Keep one pocket filled with your own cards and use the other to receive cards.

At a meeting, it is important to keep the card with you, suggesting that you are not discarding or disregarding this individual. Rather, place the business card subtly around your portfolio so that you can refer to the card and use the person's name when appropriate during the course of the meeting. Ultimately, place the business card in a respectful location. Rather than stuffing it into your wallet or dropping it loose in your briefcase, consider placing the card into your portfolio or, gentlemen, inner breast pocket.

When Should Cards Be Exchanged?

When you arrive at a meeting site, the first person who should receive your business card is the receptionist. Many people forget this individual when it comes to card exchange. This is a missed opportunity. The receptionist is the person who must announce you. Making sure the receptionist has your correct name, title, and affiliation will help smooth your arrival. By offering a card, you make it easier for that person to do his or her job. Another reason to do so: Offering a business card when you arrive is a gesture of respect. It is acknowledging that this individual is also a member of the organization with whom you endeavor to do business. By bringing the receptionist into the circle of your business call, you have acknowledged her and her important role in running the business. This is an opportunity to acknowledge and make a connection with key office support staff. Your gesture in using his or her name by referencing the badge or name plate, and becoming acquainted with him, shows respect and helps build a bond with this individual and with the company as a whole.

Ideally, business cards should be exchanged at the start of a meeting. Take this exchange seriously and pay close attention to the cards you receive. The information on these cards will help you better perform in the meeting that ensues. When you receive cards from other participants, place them around your portfolio in such as way that you can refer to them during the meeting. This will help enhance your performance. When you can refer to individuals during the meeting by name and even address specific comments to them directly based on their area of expertise, you enhance your own professional image as an individual attentive to detail. What else, do you take the time or make the effort to learn about and utilize? Bottom line: I want to do business with you!

At a networking event, business cards can be exchanged at the initial introduction or in parting. As is the case with business meetings, it is ideal to exchange cards at the earliest possible stage, so that you may make use of the information on the card to enhance the interaction. Never presume that someone wants your card. Instead, make the request of the other person: "May I ask for your card?" Then, ask again for your part: "May I offer you my card?" Asking shows that, again, you assume nothing. Never assume someone wants your business card. In fact, I have had people decline my card after offered. It is far less disruptive to have someone decline the offer of a card when it is made verbally. If the person were to decline while you were already holding your card out, that would be far more awkward. Do not presume. Show respect by asking first, thereby assuming nothing as you endeavor to establish trust and earn respect.

In some cases, it is a faux pas to request a card. Senior executives, for example, only exchange business cards with those of similar rank. If a high-ranking individual requests your card, consider this an honor; however, do not assume you will be receiving one in return.

Suppose you want to make notes on a business card you have just received? This is a common impulse, but it must be handled carefully to avoid possibly offending the other person. In Asian countries, for example, a business card is considered far more than just a piece of paper with information. It is a manifestation of one's personae. Writing on the card, therefore, is considered defacement of the person's life. Even in North America, scribbling on the back of another's business card can be off-putting to the person offering the card. Still, making notes is a smart way to gather and retain key client information. If you are going to make notes about the person whom you have just met, do so discreetly, certainly not in her presence. Make it a point to remember the information until you can more subtly make notes, out of view of the card giver.

Another situation that presents an opportunity to display an etiquette nuance: Someone asks you to call him when he returns to the country in two weeks and asks that you call him on his cell phone, which is not listed on the business card.

Question: Where do you write the cellular phone telephone number?

Answer: On the back of the business card.

However, be sure to add the nuance. Say, "Would you mind if I wrote that on the back of your business card?" This indicates that you know the etiquette, that it is not appropriate to do so because you are technically defacing his "life." This nuance serves to distinguish you in a very powerful way on many levels, because you are showing much respect and awareness.

Another situation: A person you meet would like to give you some key company information and you want to take a few notes. Doing so on her business card is a natural temptation. However, please consider this: The size of a business card is considerably small. The information about to be imparted is not. What is the perception if you begin to takes notes about this information and her firm on a little business card? That the information is insignificant. Do be aware of this possible misperception and adjust. Be sure you carry your portfolio or a quality notebook for such opportunities.

Consider this: When you are being hosted on another person's home turf, exchange of business cards should be done with ultimate discretion. You do not want to risk the possibility of insulting your host or suggesting in any way that you may be using your host's graciousness for your own personal or professional gain. In other words, you are not being hosted here to network, per say. However, opportunities do arise that enable connections, and they often crop up at unexpected times. It is a good judgment to exchange cards discreetly so as not to offend your host.

BUSINESS CARD TIPS

- Keep business cards in a quality case.
- Invest in quality business cards.
- Be sure your *name* is most prominent on the card.
- Ensure that your business cards look perfect. Bent cards or tipped edges will not reflect well on you.
- Never assume anyone wants your card; ask first.
- Never ask a high-ranking senior executive for her card. Many senior executives will only exchange cards with others of similar rank.
- Remember, the business card is a reflection of you and, the firm you represent. Create, cast, present, receive, acknowledge, and place business cards with respect and take advantage of this opportunity to shine.
- Do not write on a business card without asking first or until you are out of view of the giver.

13

Travel and International Etiquette

Question: You are a senior sales representative who wants a meeting with the president of a firm you have targeted in Japan, and you are having trouble getting through to this individual to get the appointment. How do you get the appointment with your international counterpart overseas?

Answer: The only way you will ever get a meeting with an individual overseas is through a mutually respected third party. Please know that, typically, only counterparts will meet with counterparts. To have an American company send over a lower-ranking individual to meet with the president of a company, for example, is considered an insult. Your president should be meeting with the president of the Japanese firm you have targeted.

Understanding correct protocols of global business is critical to success in today's global environment. In this era of instant communications and global travel, it is commonplace to have contacts and business opportunities around the world. The savvy business professional understands that traveling smart and researching customs and traditions of one's target country in advance of your trip is integral to functioning and thriving in today's global business arena. Successful business professionals preparing to conduct business overseas will take the time to learn about cultures and traditions of their target country in advance of their visit. Taking the time and making the effort to do so will only serve to earn you respect while simultaneously demonstrating respect for your international business counterparts' culture and traditional ways. I will address the issues of global and travel etiquette in this chapter.

In the world, there are two types of cultures known as *high context* and *low context* cultures, referring to the way persons of different cultures interact and communicate. Both cultures represent different ways of conceptualizing and communicating, including language, verbal and nonverbal communication, customs, perceived values, and perceptions regarding time and space. Herein, we will consider each.

Theorist Edward T. Hall defines culture as "man's medium; there is not one aspect of human life that is not touched and altered by culture. This means personality, how people express themselves (including shows of emotion), the way they think, how they move, how problems are solved, how their cities are planned and laid out, how transportation systems function and are organized, as well as how economic and government systems are put together and function. It is the least studied aspects of culture that influence behavior in the deepest and most subtle ways." (Hall, 1976, p. 14)

Let us consider low context cultures, such as those found in North America and much of Western Europe.

Important Characteristics of Low Context Cultures:

☞ Individualism.

☞ Logical and linear.

☞ More "here and now" oriented.

☞ Change is good; time is money.

☞ Emphasis on verbal communication versus the nonverbal message.

☞ Facts versus intuition.

☞ Direct and competitive.

☞ Freedom to openly question and challenge the status quo.

High context cultures, such as those in Asia, Africa, South America, and much of the Middle East, have different characteristics.

Important Characteristics of High Context Cultures:

☞ Collective group consensus versus individual achievement.

☞ Developing trust between individuals is paramount.

☞ Intuitive; emotions are highly valued over words or reason.

☞ Emphasis on nonverbal clues.

☞ Tradition oriented.

☞ Behavioral styles, body language, voice, tone, gestures, and sometimes even the individual's family status, hold greater significance than the

☞ Flowery language, humility, and elaborate apologies are expected.

How Culture Affects Business

Punctuality: Punctuality is expected; do not be surprised if the person with whom you are meeting arrives even 10 or 15 minutes early. Most recently in China, however, where there is much construction and traffic jams, arriving late for meetings is the norm and everyone understands why. No one considers this an insult in any way.

Titles and honorifics: Titles should always be used. The exchange of business cards is common, as are hospitality gestures such as offers of coffee or beverages. Even during the workday, hosts may offer and guests should accept beer or propose a toast with an alcoholic beverage.

Communications: It is helpful to establish bilingual business contacts before arriving. Promotional or negotiatory materials should be translated, printed before you leave, and presented in their native language. Translation services in hotels are expensive and not always reliable.

Wherever your business may take you, research the customs and travel issues before you leave, and have a person in place with whom you can consult during the trip. Do not wait until after the trip to discover your cultural faux pas. It's too late. Advance research, planning, and much preparation will serve to make travel and global business profitable.

Often, a cultural miscue can sink a carefully arranged meeting. I met a television station executive who shared with me his story of cross-cultural misunderstanding in Japan. After months of working to arrange a meeting and finally securing one, thanks to the help of a mutually respected third party, the executive arrived in Japan. At the last minute, he decided to bring his business partner, whom he hoped would be helpful in negotiations. The two were kept waiting in the reception area for more than two hours. To pass the time, they caught up on some work they had brought along.

When they were finally met and invited back into their Japanese hosts' offices, the television station executive noticed that his partner used the first name of his host in conversation and that when he sat, he did so with his feet placed on the desk of his Japanese host, ankles crossed, and the soles of his shoes facing his host.

No business was transacted that day and there was no further communication for many, many months. The television executive's attempts at follow-up phone calls, e-mails, and faxes were rebuffed. It took a full year for the executive to secure another meeting. The first thing said from the Japanese executive at the meeting was, "You know, you and I would be doing business together long before now, had it not been for that person you brought with you, to our first meeting." Cultural mistakes can cost you business.

The business of international protocol is full of important nuances. Consider the following:

☞ The only way you will get the meeting overseas is by enlisting the help of the mutually respected third party.

☞ Be prepared not to conduct business until after two or even three initial meetings. You are being evaluated as to whether or not they want to do business with you.

☞ Have an agenda and anticipate reactions and objections.

☞ Personal space is to be respected at all costs. Please know that personal space, one's "comfort zone," varies as you travel to various countries.

☞ Handshaking is standard greeting around the world. However, different countries are known for different types of handshakes. In France, one to two pumps; in Latin and Arab countries, a limp, slow handshake. In Germany, one brisk pump; in Japan, a handshake and a bow. There are three levels of bows to respect and implement: a 15%, 35%, and 50% angled bow. Lower your bow as you meet more senior executives; the most senior executive will be honored with a 50% angle bow.

☞ Touching, hugs, and embraces also vary from country to country. When receiving those from different cultures into our country, it is respect-ful to greet them in the form they are most accus-tomed. We have seen photos and footage of President Bush holding hands in the Rose Garden with visiting dignitaries from other countries. President Bush demonstrates respect for other's culture and traditions even on his own soil. This gesture is gracious, appreciated, respectful and no doubt goes a long way in terms of helping grow the relationship, which is always the goal.

☞ Kissing: The French have been credited with the "two-kiss" kiss, one kiss on either cheek. Because we are global, more people have adopted this form of greeting universally. We continue to try to adopt and adapt, out of respect and perhaps to be chic. If you are going to kiss, please know that "air kisses" are considered an affectation. Place a kiss on the cheek. Kiss from right to right, your right side to their right side. This mode of greet-ing has deep historical roots, dating back to days when knights would approach each other. They would hold up their right hand as a sign of peace and to show that they were not concealing a weapon. Handshaking and the two-cheek kiss, starting from one's right side, evolved as a direct result of this gesture. In Belgium, you can expect three kisses and there are even four kisses in other parts of the world.

☞ Attire: Emphasize quality and a conservative look. Let everything about your professional at-tire speak of professionalism and quality; be con-servative. For ladies, skirts rather than pants are still considered the most professional in the busi-ness world today here and overseas. Pearls, gold,

hosiery, classic pumps, neutral hose, closed necklines, and hemlines just above the knee or even
mid-calf are all considered most professional (For
more, see Chapter 11). There is substance to the
notion that the more senior the woman executive, the longer her hemline.

☞ Sitting: Sit focused forward, with an invisible "V"
between you and the back of the chair. Legs
should slope either to the left or to the right. If
knees or ankles are crossed, the slope again to
either side is a lovely nuance related to sitting for
women. Gentlemen should resist the urge to sit
so that their ankle rests on the opposite knee.
This body language suggests you are closed. The
crossed leg is a barrier. Also, by exposing the sole
of the foot, you risk offending your host.

☞ Business card exchange: Remember to present
and receive a business card with either two thumbs
on either corner (most formal) or one thumb on
one corner (second most formal method of business card exchange). Acknowledging the card is
the most important point of business card exchange. And then, placing the card someplace
respectful is appropriate. Please know that the
business card should not be used to list marketing information or categories and subcategories
of services and capabilities on the reverse side.
The opposite side of the business card should
only be used, if at all, for imprinting the same
information that appears on the front, only in
the giver's native language. Separate marketing materials should be printed on a separate
marketing piece for distribution.

☞ Honorifics: Do not assume a first-name basis. Always use the person's honorific until invited to do otherwise. Even then, with very senior executives, particularly in the presence of their staff and/or other guests and colleagues, use their honorific as a show of respect. If you have been given permission to address this individual by his first name, do so privately, not in a business meeting during formal negotiations.

☞ Interpreters: Have your own. Much can be lost in translation.

☞ Introduce colleagues in a professional manner. (See Chapter 3.)

☞ Have an agenda prepared, even if they do not. This will distinguish you as a professional, truly prepared for this meeting. Even if there are only a few items on this agenda, do have this prepared and distribute the meeting agenda in advance.

☞ Do much preplanning and preparation for the meeting before you go; they will. You should also anticipate reactions, objections, glitches, and where you may need to negotiate; be prepared to counter, squelch objections, conquer, and win.

☞ Be aware of subtleties in certain cultures. For example, know the Japanese will never say no. Because they are a most gracious culture and do not wish to offend they will never say the word "no." Rather, they will say, "Perhaps not at this time" or "This may not be possible." Read between the lines and understand this subtlety really means no way or "not going to happen."

☞ Gifting is a big part of international business. Be aware of colors used in wrapping gifts that may be offensive in itself, numbers that are unlucky, bows, and, of course, the gift itself. Know who and when to gift and, be careful not to over-gift.

☞ Gestures, jokes, use of slang, jargon, and addressing others by their first name too soon in the relationship can all be self-sabotage.

☞ Do try to learn some key words and phrases of the language, enough to demonstrate you have made the effort, even if your pronunciation is a bit off. This goes a long way in terms of endearing one's self to people in any country. Remember when President Kennedy was recognized as "the man who accompanied Jacqueline Kennedy to France"? Mrs. Kennedy delivered a speech, speaking fluent French. The French people were highly impressed and moved, to say the least!

☞ Hands belong on the table during the meeting and negotiations. Trust and perceptions of professionalism are at stake.

☞ There are "time" differences. Americans operate in a low-context culture and "monochromic" time theme. Time is money. "Let's do this now." In high-context and "polychromic" cultures, time is intertwined in an almost ritualistic sequence where many things must lead up to and culminate into one main event, such as a major presentation or a banquet.

☞ Entertainment is part of the international business protocol. Be prepared to reciprocate gracious offers of entertaining as a gift.

☞ Eating habits vary. Be aware that in other countries, such as China, Americans will get a big
wake-up call. They will be struck by noise levels
while dining and entertaining during dinner. There
is much slurping going on and arms we were always told did not belong on the table will rest
comfortably on the table in China. Because they
come from a history of such extreme poverty,
Chinese people let nothing go to waste and eat
everything they can, including dogs, fish eyes,
body organs, fingernails, very rare mushrooms
(a great delicacy), and rooster's feet (a lot of
bones!). Bringing your cup of noodles to your
lips and using chopsticks to almost shovel noodles
into your mouth is the norm.

I had this experience firsthand. While in Beijing, I was
hosted by the Mayor of Beijing along with several other senior
business executives at a fabulous banquet. I had my left hand
in my lap and brought noodles to my mouth with chopsticks
from the table up to my mouth as always. My Japanese partner from the United States, who was our intermediary, caught
my eye and silently demonstrated the proper way to eat the
noodles in China. He brought the bowl to his mouth, literally
pressed it against his lips and proceeded to show me how to
"shovel" noodles into my mouth all while resting the left elbow and arm on the table. I did follow suit, feeling a bit awkward yet being reassured this was how I was supposed to eat,
dining with my new Chinese friends. I thought, "If my teenage
son could see his mother now!"

Cultural differences also turn up in other settings. Take
photography. Many Chinese people love to have their picture
taken, especially with Americans. I found it was not uncommon to be randomly stopped and asked to pose for photos.
This, however, brought to light another cultural difference.

Personal space is precious and, therefore, to be respected at all costs. Touching and violating personal space, even for a photo opportunity, particularly in a business situation, is a major faux pas. After a business lunch, one of our American colleagues posed in a "group hug," arms wrapped right around the mayor's neck, with a huge, ridiculous smile. I was mortified. Everyone was mortified. The mayor graciously went along with this and never said a word, nor did anyone else. However, the American friend's name was never mentioned again nor was he invited to another function during our visit. This speaks to how effortlessly American's can self-sabotage and sabotage an entourage, even though there was preparation here. Old habits die hard. You must always be aware of your cultural environment and consider the customs while meeting with and visiting abroad.

☞ Hands: Hands belong on the desk in the meeting room, boardroom, or dining room table, not on your lap. The reason is twofold: This looks more professional and the perception is you are in control. Sitting in this way inspires trust, showing you are not hiding anything.

☞ Car/Limousine etiquette: The host is always seated to the rear right of the car or limousine. It is gracious of the host to defer the position of honor to her person of honor.

In addition to learning your destination's specific culture and traditions, there are also general travel etiquette rules to keep in mind.

Travel Time

Do not underestimate travel time in transit. Travel time is not lost time. It can be an opportune time to engage in valuable networking activities, however inadvertently. Travel anywhere in the world presents opportunities to meet others one would not normally have the opportunity to meet. Do take advantage of your travel situation. Consider the following travel tips to help achieve enhanced professional credibility:

Attire

Yes, you are preparing to spend many long hours in a commercial aircraft or train and would like to be comfortable. You prefer to dress casually. Please know that "comfortable" and "casual" can mean different things to different individuals. Because you never know who you may encounter en route, one should always dress professionally. Traveling in sweats or wrinkled blue jeans, however comfortable, does not cast the professional image you are endeavoring to portray. Men and women should dress professionally. Take time with your appearance. You are not off duty.

I have had the great fortune of meeting many professionals with whom I have developed strong business and personal relationships. I had the following travel experience I would like to share, by way of example: I arrived at my seat on a commercial aircraft in the coach section of a plane and began placing some things overhead. I noticed a suitcase resting there, a Luis Vuitton carry on. I like Luis Vuitton and looked down at my travel neighbor who was fabulously well dressed and polished; everything about him said 100% quality, professional. I offered a friendly hello and commented on his case. I told him I had just been looking at the Luis Vuitton luggage, but when I saw the price tag, I had second thoughts. He said in a very thick German accent, "If you want it, you can't think about it, you just have to do it." I sat down next to him and we exchanged some small talk. He was working and it was clear he did not care to chat, and so I took the cue.

Here it must be said, in the meantime, I had a client whose husband had asked for some au courant tips regarding the

German culture as he would be meeting with a major German production company and wanted to make sure he was dead on target with his German culture. Therefore, after hearing this gentleman's thick German accent, I wanted to take the opportunity to ask some questions and possibly learn from this clearly refined, cultured, seemingly astute individual. Perhaps he could help me better serve my client by confirming or denying questions I had regarding German culture?

I took the opportunity to open the door for discussion during beverage service. I told him I noticed his German accent and let him know I was an etiquette and protocol consultant. I gently suggested that I would appreciate any tutelage he might offer regarding the German culture. Would he have any au courrant advice to offer me pertaining to German business protocols? He was more than generous and forthcoming with information. For the remainder of the flight, he shared many insights and nuances pertaining to the German business culture and conducting business. He was also gracious enough to suggest that I might be helpful to him in explaining some nuances pertaining to American business culture. I obliged, of course. Our flight landed and we were preparing to deplane when I realized that, oddly, the topic of what business he was in never came up. So I asked. "I am sorry. What business are you in?" He told me he was a diplomat from Germany and gave me his business card, which revealed that, in fact, he was a very, very senior-level diplomat from Germany. I should have known. We developed a professional rapport and he proved to be not only a lovely gentleman, but a valuable business contact as well. I am certain that had I been wearing blue jeans and a tee shirt, sporting unkempt hair and no makeup, I would never have been able to have a conversation and the benefit of wisdom this gentleman imparted. My professional appearance and respectful demeanor helped me open the door to this business relationship.

Packing

Travel lightly. Packing coordinated separates will make packing, travel, and managing your wardrobe easier while on the road. Wheeled luggage has cut severely into tips for and jobs of those in baggage handling. Be aware that regulations regarding carry-on luggage are often subject to new security rules. Your best attempts at avoiding checked luggage might be thwarted by security issues of the day. Do you best to adhere to the latest regulations, but also know these are subject to change without notice.

Be sure to pack items that allow you to network effectively, should the opportunity arise while in travel. For example, be sure you can easily access business cards. It would not reflect well on you to meet a valuable business prospect on the plane only to have to admit all your business cards are packed away in your luggage, which is in the baggage hold. Similarly, carry a portfolio or a similarly professional writing accoutrement and quality pen. When I was able to make the business connection with my diplomatic neighbor, I noticed he had been writing on his leather portfolio with his quality pen. Similarly, when I asked if I might take a few notes and he agreed, I was able to pull out my portfolio and quality pen. Certainly, my impression might not have been the same if I had pulled out a composition notebook similar to the one my teenage son uses, or if I took notes on a cocktail napkin. Because I was prepared, I believe I was able to present a professional, credible image.

Food

Given the airline industry and food today, it is wise to pack or purchase something to eat en route. Pack or purchase easy-to-eat food. Be aware that security restrictions apply to beverages and even ladies makeup.

Security Issues

The best way to avoid having security issues hamper your trip is by planning what not to wear in order to breeze through security. Online airline regulations are available. Be aware of items such as jewelry, belt buckles, or anything metallic that might trigger the security detector. Try to wear shoes you can easily slip on and off. Know that your appearance will also be considered by and have an impact on security personnel, who are trained to scrutinize travelers. Dress as the business professional you are.

Security issues also apply to technology items you may be carrying. By now, most experienced business travelers know they may be asked to boot up a lap top or otherwise demonstrate the use of a technology item for security personnel. It is not unheard of for a security officer to insist that a technology item be x-rayed or checked as baggage rather than carried on the plane. Be prepared for this and check to ensure any critical software or other items are stored in such a way that they will travel safely as well. You can purchase travel bags specifically designed for high-technology items.

Be Courteous

It sounds simple. While traveling, be especially courteous. Travel time, fatigue, and delays all contribute to high anxiety and short tempers. Airline personnel are under tremendous pressure to perform their duties and responsibilities. Although admittedly, some get caught up in the "power," exhibiting rude behavior, hostility, and even arrogance, as I, myself, have witnessed. Especially during these times, it is advantageous to all concerned to make an extra effort to demonstrate the utmost respect for authority figures and airline personnel and, show appreciation for any and all services performed on your behalf, large or small. Please, thank you, excuse me, and sorry go a very long way in terms of appreciation.

These simple, most frequently said words in any language, go a long way toward helping you advance and instill civility in an otherwise potentially explosive situation when sour looks prevail and tempers flare. A positive attitude and projecting positive energy is noticed, and you will continue to get back what you give. Upon arrival at your final destination, you may find even the desk clerk more willing to upgrade your room because you politely explained why the first room was unsatisfactory. Being courteous to and respectful of others is noticed, appreciated, and contagious.

Tipping

Tipping often baffles even the most savvy business professional. When you think about it, a tip means: "to insure promptness." In other words, tipping is critical to ensure good service. While the protocols of tipping during travel can be confusing, no one wants to come across as an inexperienced traveler. To come across as a seasoned travel professional, here are a few tipping do's to consider.

First, there are no absolutes in determining who, when, and how much to tip. You may feel free to offer the gesture to anyone you would like. This said, tipping the manager, owner, or proprietor would be insulting, as they earn a respectful wage and are not dependent on their tips as income. However, generally speaking, any service provider should be tipped.

Tipping in a Restaurant

The maître d': There is no official rule regarding tipping the maitre d' and tipping is not expected. Rather, this is up to the discretion of the guest. If you feel you have been treated with respect, made to feel special and even perhaps like family, then a tip would be appropriate and appreciated. Amounts: $10 or $20 is appropriate, although in an upscale restaurant or hotel, $50 and $100 is not unusual. In many cases, the tip can have a lasting impact on your experience at this restaurant.

How much are you willing to tip to help build a solid relationship? The higher the tip, the better the relationship, not only with the maitre d', but also among every other service professional in the restaurant, because they come to know you then as a "good tipper" and will most certainly take good care of you and your guests at future occasions. This is an important element to remember if you intend to become a regular at any establishment.

Sommelier: Encountering a true sommelier these days in the United States is rare. However, when this occurs, here are some tipping guidelines: As a general guide, tip a percentage of the bottle price; 20% is appropriate. Sometimes it is logistically challenging to tip the sommelier, because he may not be accessible when you are preparing to pay the bill. Restaurants recognize this and therefore often pay the sommelier a higher hourly rate. If you are unable to tip the sommelier, do not panic. Tipping this individual remains discretionary.

Captain and wait staff: The captain and wait staff frequently share tips; plan on 18% to 22% of your bill. If you are in doubt, simply write on your check: "Gratuity: 22% split among captain and wait staff." You may tip more for better service, less accordingly.

Common Tipping Questions

Question: When the bill is excessive due to the cost of a bottle of wine or champagne, should the percentage guidelines be adjusted accordingly, when calculating the tip?

Answer: This is a highly emotionally charged issue among restaurateurs, staff, and patrons. Restaurateurs will suggest that if you can afford the $500 bottle, you should be able to afford the 20 to 22% tip. Patrons will argue that the service provider is performing precisely the same duties and functions for the $60 bottle as the $500 bottle, and so they should not be tipped so exorbitantly. One restaurant, which has been in business forever, took control of this issue and decided to make a rule: No more than $30 would be accepted as gratuity for any bottle, regardless of its price.

Question: Is it appropriate to leave a very small tip for poor service?

Answer: Naturally, if service was poor, one would leave a reduced tip. However, one should always communicate the reason for the lower gratuity directly to the manager and/or wait staff directly. Leaving a lower tip without communicating the reason is completely inappropriate and would simply lead the establishment and the server to believe that you are cheap.

Quesion: If I order a glass of water at the bar and there is no charge, should I leave a tip?

Answer: Even though there is no check you must understand that the bartender has taken as much time and provided to you the same level of service and personal attention as if you had ordered any other beverage. You should also be sensitive to the fact that by taking up a seat at the bar you are potentially costing the bartender revenue. For both these reasons a tip is required when ordering even water while sitting at the bar.

Question: Do coat check personnel receive a tip?

Answer: Yes. Anywhere between $1 and $5 per coat is appropriate, depending on the establishment. Special items such a mink or other fur suggests a higher tip is in order.

Other Tipping Tips

☞ Skycap: $2 to $3 per bag. Do not forget this individual. You may never see your bags again!

☞ Bell staff: If your luggage is on wheels, you may handle this yourself. If the bell staff handles your bags for you, $2 to $5 per bag is appropriate again, depending on the establishment, the luggage, and attitude. Keep in mind that bell staff often do more than just carry your bags. This individual provides you with information about your room, the hotel, services, and even activities in the area. Certainly, other additional duties performed, willingness to assist, and attitude deserve an acknowledgement. The personal interaction here is as important as the physical assist. It is interesting to note that bell staff have shared with me that the more they use a guest's name, the higher their tip!

☞ The doorman: $2 to $5 per bag, again depending on the establishment and attitude. For the doorman who hails you a cab, depending upon traffic, level of difficulty, and weather considerations, $2 to $5 is appropriate. Going above and beyond hailing you a cab calls for $10 or more.

☞ The valet: Shoeshines warrant a $2 to $5 tip.

☞ Dry cleaning: A delivery charge is included in the price and therefore a tip is not necessary.

☞ Room service: Many hotels have initiated a mandatory delivery charge on room service. This negates the need to tip, and your server should inform you that the gratuity has already been added to your bill. When in doubt, always ask.

☞ Valet storage of luggage and other articles: $2 to $5 per item.

☞ The concierge: Tipping the concierge varies by location. The American versus European versions of the concierge are different and have an altogether different tipping philosophy. European concierges rely almost exclusively on their tips for income. American concierges are almost always salaried individuals. One would not tip a concierge here, in America, for doing his job, such as making a restaurant reservation, securing a theatre ticket, or providing directions. However, if the concierge performs unusual duties for you, above and beyond the norm, one typically develops a very personal rapport with that concierge and should absolutely tip that individual accordingly at the end of your stay. That cash amount should be placed in an envelope, along with a personal note of thanks, and placed directly in the person's hand, along with your warm and sincere thanks. This amount is entirely discretionary. While $20 is never wrong, $50, $100 or more, depending on what the person actually did to assist you, is entirely appropriate.

☞ Housekeeping: The appropriate tip for housekeeping services is $2 to $3 per room night. The general rule suggests the level of tipping for housekeeping personnel would not vary regardless if you were staying at a Four Seasons or Ritz-Carlton or a local motel. However, clearly, one needs to use common sense in applying this rule. If you were staying in a local motel with a room rate of $30 per night and little in the way of housekeeping services, $1 per night would certainly be acceptable. At the other end of the spectrum, at an upscale hotel where the room rate may exceed $400 to $500 per night and housekeeping services would include substantially more services, such as turn-down service, fresh towels, and so on, one would likely want to exceed the $2 per night guide.

A cautionary word here: It is sometimes dangerous to leave any cash in your room and assume it will reach the housekeeping staff. Too many staff members have access to your room for you to be assured that the tip will reach the appropriate person. In fact, it could even end up going to a member of the housekeeping staff who just came on duty. The safe course here is to hand your tip, placed in an envelope, along with a brief, handwritten note on hotel stationery, directly to the housekeeper who has been caring for you and your room. In the event that you do not see your housekeeper, you should leave the envelope with a hotel staff, with your service provider's name on the envelope.

☞   Engineering: Tipping is not necessary; these are salaried individuals.

Please note that tipping practices vary from country to country. It is advised that you research the country you are visiting to find out local practices. Should you feel compelled to do something more, as always, writing a letter acknowledging the extra efforts of this individual to their superior is most appreciated and helps that person during job performance reviews and other employee recognition moments.

International Business

Travel, tipping, and protocols vary widely among regions and countries. It is wise to have researched these in advance. Wherever your business may take you, research the customs and travel issues before you leave, and have an individual in place with whom you can consult during the trip. Waiting until after the trip is over to discover your cultural faux pas is too late. Advance planning makes travel and global business profitable.

HOW TO RECOVER IF...

...you make a faux pas during an international trip.

Apologize as soon as you recognize the error. Then, apologize some more, particularly if you are in a high context country in which open and extensive apologies are the norm.

Acknowledge the faux pas. Make an honest effort to learn and correct the appropriate protocol; this will go a long way, indeed, toward forgiveness and help ensure you are ultimately received in a favorable light.

Additional Resources

Books

Alldessandra, Tonoy, Ph.D., and M.J. O'Connor, Ph.D. *Know Your Customer. The Platinum Rule*.

Fisher, Seymour, Ph.D. *Body Language*.

Hall, Edward T *Beyond Culture*.

———. *The Hidden Dimension*.

———. *The Silent Language*.

Miller, Robert B., and Gary A. Willum, with Alden M. Hayash. *The 5 Paths to Persuasion*.

Riso, Don Richard, and Russ Hudson. *Discovering your Personality Type*.

Tieger, Paul D. and Barbara Barron. *Speedreading People*.

Walters, Barbara. *How to Talk with Practically Anybody about Practically Anything*.

Weill, Sandy. *The Real Deal: My Life in Business and Philanthropy*.

Websites

Business Travel News. A publication focused on the news and trends in global business travel.
www.btnmag.com

DISC. A series of assessments and guidelines designed to improve interpersonal relationships, teamwork and productivity. Based on the research of psychologist William Moulton Marston.
www.discprofile.com

Executive Planet Inc. A company and web site devoted to the intricacies of international business travel.
www.executiveplanet.com

Presentations Magazine. A business publication devoted to the skills and technologies of stellar presentations.
www.presentations.com

Toastmasters International. An excellent resource for those endeavoring to improve public speaking skills.
www.toastmasters.org/

Index

216

About the Author

Judith Bowman, who founded Protocol Consultants International in 1993, is one of the country's leading authorities on corporate etiquette, international protocol, dining, networking, behavioral styles, and presentation skills. Ms. Bowman provides training and seminars on issues of corporate etiquette and professional presence to many Fortune 500 firms and is also a corporate keynote speaker and presenter on professional presence and protocol.

Ms. Bowman is a graduate of Boston College and has pursued studies in effective business communication at Harvard University. In 1993 and 1995, she earned certifications in child, teen, and adult etiquette, as well as corporate etiquette, international protocol, and dining savvy. She has been active in numerous professional organizations, including the World Affairs Council, American Women in Radio and Television, Women in Technology International (WITI), Boston Women Communicators, numerous chambers of commerce and business roundtables, New England Speaker's Association, New England Human Resource Association, Greater Boston

Concierge Association, Women's Business Network, and the Women's Educational and Industrial Union.

Judith Bowman served as host of *Etiquette First* and *Mind Your Manners,* weekly features on New England Cable News for a combined total of four years. She appears on local and national radio and television shows extensively, including Fox News, UPN 38/WBZ, *Chronicle, CBS This Morning*, the TV Food Network, and more.

Ms. Bowman authors a weekly etiquette column entitled *Everyday Etiquette* and for the past six years has syndicated throughout New England by the Pulitzer Prize-winning Eagle Tribune Publishing Company.

Articles and quotes by Ms. Bowman have appeared in *Forbes* magazine, *CFO Magazine, CNN Everyday Money, The Financial Advisor, The Boston Business Journal, Women's Business, Mass High Tech, Los Angeles Times, Business Week, Banker & Tradesman, Self* magazine, *The Boston Globe, The Boston Herald, The Restaurant Review, The Boston Courant, Elegant Wedding,* and many others.

Ms. Bowman is the executive producer of her corporate training video entitled *Executive Etiquette–First Impressions, Volume I,* and recently she has released her new DVD dining video titled *DINING 101.*

Ms. Bowman is known for her ability to help students and professionals further distinguish themselves in business, and to help them to develop, cultivate, maintain, and grow strong relationships.